W0081444

0 14

# Raising Brows

# Raising Brows

## MY STORY OF BUILDING A
## BILLION-DOLLAR BEAUTY EMPIRE

## Anastasia Soare

PORTFOLIO ~ PENGUIN

Portfolio / Penguin
An imprint of Penguin Random House LLC
1745 Broadway, New York, NY 10019
penguinrandomhouse.com

PORTFOLIO and PORTFOLIO with javelin thrower design are registered
trademarks of Penguin Random House LLC.

Most Portfolio books are available at a discount when purchased in quantity for sales
promotions or corporate use. Special editions, which include personalized covers, excerpts,
and corporate imprints, can be created when purchased in large quantities. For more
information, please call (212) 572-2232 or email specialmarkets@penguinrandomhouse.com.
Your local bookstore can also assist with discounted bulk purchases using the
Penguin Random House corporate Business-to-Business program. For assistance in
locating a participating retailer, email B2B@penguinrandomhouse.com.

Illustrations on pages 75 and 80, top, by Anastasia Soare. All other images
from the collection of Anastasia Beverly Hills.

Book design by Alissa Rose Theodor

LIBRARY OF CONGRESS CATALOGING-IN-PUBLICATION DATA
Names: Soare, Anastasia, author.
Title: Raising brows : my story of building a billion-dollar beauty empire / Anastasia Soare.
Description: New York, NY : Portfolio/Penguin, [2025]
Identifiers: LCCN 2025019419 | ISBN 9798217044542 (hardcover) |
ISBN 9798217044559 (ebook) | ISBN 9798217181377 (international edition)
Subjects: LCSH: Soare, Anastasia | Beauty operators—United States—Biography |
Businesswomen—United States—Biography | Romanians—United States—Biography |
Cosmetics industry—United States | Eyebrows |
LCGFT: Autobiographies
Classification: LCC TT955.S63 A3 2025
LC record available at https://lccn.loc.gov/2025019419

Printed in the United States of America
1st Printing

The authorized representative in the EU for product safety and compliance is
Penguin Random House Ireland, Morrison Chambers, 32 Nassau Street,
Dublin D02 YH68, Ireland, https://eu-contact.penguin.ie.

*For Claudia and my mother,*
*who are my everything*

## Dedication

This book is dedicated to those striving for a better life and brighter future for themselves and their families, especially immigrants. They arrive with dreams in their hearts and work relentlessly to turn those dreams into reality. Their resilience and dedication are truly inspiring. To the younger generation born here, remember that someone in your family made significant sacrifices to pave the way for you. Always honor their dedication and determination, as they are the foundation upon which your opportunities are built.

# CONTENTS

# Raising Brows

# PART ONE

# Believe in your dreams.
# Don't give up.

If I could give my daughter three things, they would be
the confidence to always know her self-worth, the ability
to know how deeply she is loved, and the strength to
chase her dreams. I wish that for all of you too.

# What Makes You Feel Beautiful Makes You Powerful

I have lived two lives: one in Romania, the other in America. My early life in Romania shaped who I am, forging my values around hard work, determination, and resilience. These qualities revealed the importance of endurance and inspired me to always have courage to reach for more. My second life in America put everything I had learned in Romania to the test and then some— in America I built my confidence, honed my craft, listened to my voice above anyone else, and found success on a scale I never thought imaginable. What unifies both my lives is belief. A belief in destiny. A belief in myself.

People often ask me what the secret to achievement is. Of course, it has a lot to do with working hard, building authentic connections, striving for excellence in every pursuit, being determined, and always doing more than the job at hand. Principles by which I live. But it is also about something less tangible and more magical that begins when you cultivate a particular attitude that drives you forward. For me, it is an unshakable belief that whispers in my ear from the minute I get up to when I go to sleep that says . . . *You* can do anything. I have always believed this, and it has been the foundation and heartbeat of all I have accomplished.

I am the founder and CEO of Anastasia Beverly Hills, though people often refer to me as the Queen of Eyebrows—and I am very proud when they do. I have been lucky to know some of the most beautiful and impactful people in the entertainment industry. It is incredibly gratifying to me that, over the course of my career, my work has been appreciated by well-known people such as Jennifer Aniston, Garcelle Beauvais, Victoria Beckham, Hailey Bieber, Naomi Campbell, Cardi B, Priyanka Chopra, Amal Clooney, Penélope Cruz, Laura Dern, Cameron Diaz, Megan Fox, Bethenny Frankel, Paris Hilton, Kendall Jenner, Kris Jenner, Kylie Jenner, Khloé Kardashian, Kim Kardashian, Kourtney Kardashian, Gayle King, Heidi Klum, Eva Longoria, Jennifer Lopez, Elle Macpherson, Madonna, Maria Menounos, Michelle Obama, Michelle Pfeiffer, Claudia Schiffer, Lorraine Schwartz, Stephanie Seymour, Sharon Stone, Charlize Theron, Sofía Vergara, Serena Williams, Rita Wilson, Oprah Winfrey, Reese Witherspoon, and more.

Equally important is that my work has been appreciated by the thousands of individuals who have come to my Beverly Hills salon and the millions of people who use my techniques to shape their eyebrows in their homes around the world. When people use my products, I feel like they are embracing my values, my craft, and my hard work. They are also celebrating all the employees, partners, customers, and influencers who have been loyal and loud champions of Anastasia Beverly Hills. Most of all, my success is a validation of all the many challenges I had to overcome in being a first-generation immigrant.

You might have heard me say that I invented eyebrows. Of course, people always had eyebrows! However, I do not think that anyone else had ever thought about them the way that I did. I recognized a need that served my clients and a void in the beauty industry that created an entirely new category.

Using makeup is just like painting a portrait: The goal is to create harmony and the illusion of balance and proportion while still embracing your unique features. I learned in an art class in Romania that painters could change the entire look of a face just by changing the eyebrow shape. Leonardo da Vinci used the golden ratio, a measure that creates perfect proportion and balance, in his paintings. The human eye is encoded with the ability to recognize this particular ratio as pleasing.

I began to apply this scientific formula to my client's faces. Taking this concept off the canvas and onto the brows of real-life people was as game-changing for the person in my chair at the salon as it was for me. When the three zones of the face are equally balanced, you create a harmony that is perceived as beautiful. My golden ratio method produces a powerful transformation that enhances people's natural features. I loved seeing the effect this had on women's confidence. It was then that I realized that what makes you feel beautiful makes you powerful. And I loved making women feel powerful. From there, I listened to my client's needs and utilized my technical art training to create products for the perfect Anastasia brows, and many more makeup products afterward.

The journey from an immigrant who didn't speak English to a woman driven by a defining idea to CEO of the globally successful

Anastasia Beverly Hills had twists and turns of extreme joy and difficulty. That is why I am writing this book. Not to tell you how to sculpt an eyebrow or build a beauty company of your own, but to share everything I've learned about success in business and in life so that your own path to success will be as smooth as possible. I'm sharing my story to inspire and encourage you to listen to yourself and your dreams, to tune in to your instincts and beliefs to create a life full of wonder and accomplishment—whatever those things mean for you. I believe everyone has a special contribution to make. Maybe you already know what that ability is, and you have a dream in mind but you're lacking the courage to act on it. Or maybe you're still figuring it out. Either way, I want to help you find and unlock it. I believe you can.

## Where You Come from Doesn't Define Who You Are

No matter where you come from, you can change the course of your life. If you don't believe that statement, I am the proof. For as long as I can remember, I wanted to do something with my life that would make a difference. Under Communism in Romania, life was hard. Food was scarce, and people would line up for hours in the cold just to receive one chicken or maybe just a few potatoes to feed their families. It was a day-to-day grind. People had to exist in survival mode. I had other plans for my life. My imagination and outlook were expansive, and I felt deep in my bones that there must be more to life than surviving from day to day. I watched bootleg copies of *Pretty Woman* and *Beverly Hills Cop* and dreamed of moving to America, the land of opportunity. I visualized myself walking down Rodeo Drive and feeling the California sunshine on my skin. When you believe in your dream

hard enough, you will do what it takes to make it come true. After many years of struggle in order to leave Romania, I finally
arrived at the beginning. An immigrant in a new land, running
to catch up to those already here. Running toward my American
dream.

I didn't know what I was going to do with my life right away,
but there was always something inside that kept pushing me forward. Even when I was called crazy for trying to open a salon and
the landlord laughed at the idea that a business could be built on
shaping brows. Even when the bank would not give me a loan. Or
when I drove a rickety old Ford station wagon as big as my bedroom from where I could afford to live to my salon in Beverly
Hills, two hours each way over a desolate canyon road. The car
was so broken down that garage valets would not take the keys.
It seemed that both the car and I were fueled by hope and little
miracles.

Years later, I received a personal invitation from First Lady
Michelle Obama to attend the annual White House Christmas
party. This invitation was a testament to how far I had come in
my journey and marked a significant milestone in my career. It
was truly one of the greatest days of my life. I had the honor of
shaping the First Lady's brows for a while, which made the experience even more special. Being able to work with such a remarkable and inspiring figure added depth to an already unforgettable
occasion.

The night of the party, near several fragrant Christmas trees
laden with ornaments and under an archway draped with more
decorative garlands, I stood under the Presidential Seal. My
daughter, Claudia, took a photo. It is still one of my most trea-
sured images. I've experienced many milestones in growing my

business, which I call my *Oscar moments*—having now lived half of my life in Beverly Hills and Hollywood. But this was something else. It was almost indescribable. I had been an immigrant who arrived with nothing. Now I stood wearing a beautiful gold evening gown under the Presidential Seal in the White House. I thought about the skinny girl from Romania who hoped for a new life, and about all the people around the world who still long for freedom and for the limitless possibility this country can offer. This was more than a moment; it was my greatest achievement.

I am living the American dream. If I can make my dreams come true, so can you. You can have your own Oscar moments. No matter your age, there are still possibilities ahead for you. Opportunity exists if you can see it, put in the hard work, and take action. It might take all your bravery, creativity, and stamina to find out and act on your talent, but that is where magic is found.

## Passion Is Action Amplified

The way to find your passion is to take action. I did not know that beauty would become my passion. I had accomplished my dream to leave Romania and to go to America, but I didn't know what the next step would be. I had no master plan to build a beauty company. I just kept following the path as it unfolded before me. I just kept doing. At the salon, every time I finished shaping a client's brows, I would hand her a mirror so she could see the results. The delight that lit up her face at seeing herself look her best as well as the confidence this gave her was thrilling to me. It filled me with huge satisfaction and joy. I helped someone! I wanted to keep doing it forever. And it is still my favorite work.

I became obsessed with figuring out how to do my work better and better. I offered the eyebrow service for free for many years to master my skills. I worked seven days a week to learn everything I could about how to run a business and serve my clients. I asked each woman who sat in my chair the same question: "How can I help you?" As I helped them, they helped me to grow. They became my circle of support. Everyone has something to teach you if you are open to it and are not afraid to ask. I found out many years later that this is called the Benjamin Franklin effect, because Franklin had discovered a psychological truth that exchanging favors makes people want to assist each other more. In listening to what my clients needed and wanted, I figured out how to create products to keep their brows groomed between sessions. That is how my first brow kit came about, and my product business was born. Through doing, it became my passion.

When you find something that you are good at, keep doing it. Don't give up. Don't worry about the money or the grand vision—they will come. Positive feedback will fuel your passion for the work and your desire to continue. When you apply discipline, resourcefulness, mastery, and energy, your passion will amplify and opportunity will find you. And when you hit a road bump, trust that you can figure it out.

I always liked figuring things out. When I was growing up in Constanța, an ancient Romanian port city on the Black Sea, many young girls would play with dolls. Instead I would visit my uncle and marvel at his work. I loved to walk down the bumpy cobbled street to my uncle's house. He was a very skilled and sought-after carpenter. I would watch his big, gnarled hands delicately chisel a perfect form from what had been just a piece of wood. It seemed wonderful to me that from seemingly nothing something beautiful could be shaped and designed. He showed me that there is always another way of seeing an object, or a problem, or a challenge. There is always a solution. And figuring out that solution is what propels me to continue to invent and innovate to this day.

## Creating Your Big Life

Most entrepreneurs, inventors, and dreamers will tell you that they walked down a long road, making many mistakes before they achieved what to others seems like an overnight success. My own journey did not unfold in perfect precision. I didn't always get everything right. I've made smart moves, and I've made million-dollar mistakes, and I've learned equally from both. I'm telling my story, the ups and downs, so you can share in the valuable lessons and the magic I discovered along the way. I learned in the trenches how to create something from nothing. I spent my childhood listening to stories of endings and difficult beginnings, of labor and loss. I spent my adult life redesigning the pattern and changing my destiny. With the right mindset, I know it's possible to turn passion into action and transform your life. It is my hope that every dreamer will find something in these pages that resonates with them, whether an aspiring entrepreneur or not.

My wish for you is to live your fullest and best life. I consider it my purpose now to support other women to thrive, grow, and succeed—just as I was supported at pivotal moments. I know how important it is to hear the stories of those who walked the same steps before you, how they managed all the pathways and pitfalls.

I believe the best gift that you can give to yourself and to the world is the gift of being authentically who you are, living your

WHAT MAKES YOU FEEL BEAUTIFUL MAKES YOU POWERFUL

purpose despite obstacles and challenges. This magic is already inside you if you dare to listen to it. You may have a family who does not understand your spirit, live in a small town that feels restrictive, or have had painful experiences as a child. You may come from privileged circumstances or have no money at all. If you limit your thinking, you will limit your opportunities. If you change your mindset, you *can* change your life. I do not mean this in a trite way or as an Instagram meme.

Your mind is a powerful tool. It is an energetic pulse that powers your actions. Your mindset is your jet fuel through life. It's not finite or fixed but ever capable of growth and change—a wave, not a wall. It's that electricity that makes your soul sing when you say to yourself, "I want my life to be more. I want it to have meaning. I want my life to unfold differently from the lives I see around me."

You can tell me all the ways you cannot do the thing you're dreaming of.

*I don't know how to start a business.*
*I don't have a college degree or an MBA.*
*I don't speak English; no one understands me when I talk.*
*I don't have contacts who can help me.*
*I don't have money.*
*I am an immigrant, new to this country.*
*I am too old.*
*I am scared.*

I have been in the same place. I have felt uncertainty and financial lack. I know what it's like to lose relationships and to leave family behind. I had many hard years and had to make many hard choices to get to today. It is not easy to hold on to your big dreams when you feel that your surroundings whittle them away to something small and uninspiring.

It is fear that keeps us standing still. I have felt that fear too. But you do not need to give in to it. Rather than think *What if people don't accept me? What if I make a mistake? What if my idea doesn't work? What if I try and I fail?*, ask yourself, *What if I succeed?*

"Our deepest fear is not that we are inadequate," wrote Marianne Williamson in *A Return to Love*. "Our deepest fear is that we are powerful beyond measure."

I believe this power is inside all of us and we can tune in to it. Every morning in the quiet before starting my day, I connect into that force to reset and recharge. I say to myself, "I can, I can, I can, and I will, I will, I will. Today, I will do something, however small, that moves toward my dreams." I will draw for ten minutes. I will learn part of a new computer program. I will make the day easier for someone else by giving them my care and attention. It does not matter how old you are, it is never too late to start. I was already thirty when I took my first job at a salon, my entrée into the beauty business, and almost forty when I started my own salon that led me to where I am today.

We all have a loop of negative fear-talk in our heads that holds us back. It tricks us into feeling safe. We might think that remaining still is safe, but that can be much worse than moving forward with gusto—like standing on a train station platform watching the trains arrive and depart without you. You will never know what opportunities might have come your way if you had only taken a chance to jump on a train and ride it to its destination, to your destiny. Think about what you want and just start.

I am not saying it is easy, but you are not alone. In sharing my story, I have also drawn out a lesson from each stage of it, high-lighting what I've learned about business and life. Take these principles that have been integral to my success and use them to build your own big life. They worked for me, and I know they will work for you too.

## You got this.
## Are you ready?

# CHAPTER ONE

# Beginnings

**To see far is one thing, going there is another.**

—Constantin Brâncuși, Romanian artist

My drive to succeed was forged by my family and by growing up in Romania. I am told that both trauma and positivity can be passed down generationally. I believe that my optimism and my grit are in my DNA. Many people today are unable to trace their family history back more than a generation. If you can't, that's OK, you can build your own narrative. If you do know your family history, there is something to learn about yourself from the stories of your past. I learned that I came from a long line of survivors.

My family story begins with my grandfather Andrei Mangri. What happened to him is the foundation of everything my family is and everything I became. It is an immigrant story. I lived it myself when I picked up and started over in another country.

My grandfather was a Macedonian who grew up in Albania. He immigrated to Romania at the turn of the last century, as it was the land of opportunity for Eastern Europe. Bucharest, the capital, was even considered the "Paris of the East." My grandfather was a boy during World War I and lost everything, including his parents. As a young man, he went to Romania in search of a better life for his family. He brought with him his wife, children, and entire extended family, including his sister, cousins, and a beloved aunt who had supported him and who he would support for the rest of her life. They settled in the countryside near Constanța, a port city on the Black Sea. There he built a large house surrounded by many acres of farmland, raising animals and crops. He began to prosper.

When he served in World War II, my grandmother ran the farm. She managed it on her own, raising my mother and her siblings with the scrappy philosophy: *Work hard, don't complain, figure it out.* Today we might call this tough love. My mother passed these traits on to me, and in turn, I passed them to my daughter.

By the time I was born, my parents had their own home with a busy tailor business in the front rooms, just down the street from the rest of the family. The Macedonian community was very tight-knit, as immigrant communities often are. We dressed slightly different from the native Romanians and ate foods made with different recipes. There were always loud family gatherings: dinners, weddings, and celebrations with my grandparents, aunts, uncles, cousins. If you can visualize *My Big Fat Greek Wedding*, it was very much like that.

When the Communist Party gained control of the country in 1947, everything changed. It was as if the sun slowly dimmed across Romania: The light seemed to shift from gold to gray. The government seized private property from landowners. The land, the animals, the big family house my grandfather had built from the ashes of his own impoverished background were all confiscated.

He moved into the city of Constanța. There, on a smaller property, he built three houses for his extended family. These were soon confiscated too, the houses torn down and replaced by a row of concrete utilitarian government apartments. He and his family were assigned small apartments in a building nearby. His apartment was on the fourth floor, with no elevator. He was eighty-six at the time.

He lived until he was ninety-two. Working on a farm had made him physically robust. Walking up and down the stairs kept him agile late in life. But his mental discipline was his enduring legacy to us. My grandfather believed that you could control your own thoughts. Much before it was popularized, he meditated every day. He was meticulous about his clothes, his food, and his mindset.

By 1975, ten years after Nicolae Ceaușescu had come to power, the Paris of the East was gone. In its place were shortages of food, heat, and individual freedom. Winters were cold; we were told to wear our clothes to bed. There were harsh penalties for those who tried to protest or fight. People just tried to survive. Through this, my grandfather's ever-present *komboloi* (prayer beads) kept him steady. He would endure no matter what was thrown at him, even though the loss all around was palpable. He was like one of the mighty granite rocks that jutted out from the coast onto the Black Sea. He stood strong and immovable even when battered by a turbulent tide.

My grandfather and I had a special bond, two rebels at heart. He had a small old radio that he kept in a tiny in corner of his room. We used to close the drapes, lock the door, and listen to the Voice of America broadcast together. We were so isolated in Romania that this was the only way we could hear what was happening in the outside world; everything on our TV and radio stations was Communist propaganda. My grandfather and I used to huddle in that corner, listen to the broadcast, and talk. He would say, "Sia, I made a big mistake. I should have immigrated to America instead of Romania. You should go to America." I think he put that seed in my head, because from a very early age I knew I wanted to go to America. Later, when my husband said it would be difficult to be an immigrant, I didn't listen. My grandfather's words always stayed with me.

I am not sure exactly when it bubbled into my conscious thought, but through my grandfather's example, I began to understand that your mind, your heart, and your spirit are your fortress. No one else has access. You have control over what you think and how you react to challenges. I would need this mindset to sustain me as I made my way out of Romania. After my husband sought political asylum in America, it held me together when I was interrogated for hours by the secret police alone in a sterile room or when our home was regularly raided. They were looking for anything they considered contraband—money, jewelry, gold, dollars, extra food. And when I waited three long and difficult years for a passport before I could embark on a plane to freedom.

My grandfather's ability to keep going taught me that no matter what is happening around you, only you have power over your mindset. Only you can decide what will give you meaning. And once you make that decision, every action you take, whether personally or in business, needs to move you toward making that life happen.

# Believe in the Possible, Even in Impossible Situations

It was during this time of sweeping change in Romania that my personal world was also turned upside down. My father died suddenly in 1969. My mother, Victoria, who was only thirty-five at the time, was left with practical concerns. My parents were still quietly tailoring in our home even though private enterprise was no longer officially allowed. Now she wondered how she would be able to provide for us on her own.

"There's no time to cry," she told me. She sat on the edge of my bed, pulling her beige wool cardigan around her. I cried in her arms. We nestled in together. I looked at her face, usually rosy, now pale and drawn. Whatever despair she felt was locked away deep inside with no key. There were no tears. She refused to give in to grief. We had to get on with living. I stopped crying and sat quietly with her. Her uncanny strength was calming, inspiring.

"Anastasia, you'll help me in the shop," she said, simply.

"Mom, I'm only twelve. I don't know how to do this." I didn't feel ready for such grown-up responsibility.

"You're smart, Sia, I will teach you everything." She always spoke in such a forceful way that you believed what she said was true. Her confidence began to persuade me. I began to think that maybe I could do this. And then I remembered how my days were usually occupied.

"What about school?" I reminded her. She was quiet for a moment before replying.

"You'll work after school," she said simply.

We looked away from the other, staring into opposite corners of the small room. We were together but each alone facing the unknown future. I snuggled into her, laying my head down on her lap. I knew that nothing further would be said. From then on when I came home from school, I would sit behind a small table my mother set up for me among the sewing machines. My school homework melded with my shopwork. I was young but I could learn. It was the beginning of my business education.

## Don't Let Limited Thinking Limit Your Opportunities

My mother was an entrepreneur at a time when most women didn't own businesses, in a country where private enterprise was forbidden. She always believed that anything was possible, and she never felt fear. This might seem quite amazing, but she was, after all, her mother's daughter: *Work hard, don't complain, figure it out.* Her father was the proud rock who would remain solid and strong no matter what came at him. Fear was not a part of the mindset she inherited, so it was not instilled in her. Our family believed there was an answer to every question, if you thought about it long enough. She would figure out a way for us to survive.

Her solution was creative and bold. She realized that despite living with rations, women still cared about how they looked. Her own mother had told her that during WWII, women had scrimped and scrounged their way to their red lipstick. There were no department stores at this time. Shoes and clothes had to be custom-made. Few people had the skill to create anything that looked at all fashionable. My mother still had the sewing machines in our front room and knew several women who could sew. She recognized there were some women in the community who were in the position to offer support.

My mother put the word out to the wives of high-ranking officials: She would keep them looking good in the latest styles. Ships docking at the port brought outside culture to us for the right price. Through her connections, my mother managed to get a smuggled, worn copy of *Vogue* magazine's *Vogue Pattern Book*, the fashion bible for American and European women. She used this as her inspiration and style guide. The old adage "Happy wives, happy lives" applied just as well then as now. The wives kept coming and my mother kept working. The officials ignored the business.

Every day when I came home from school, I would perch myself on the little wooden stool behind my worktable. There would always be a woman standing next to me waiting her turn to consult with my mother, her face animated with a sense of excitement and expectation that something out of the ordinary was going to happen. My mother would ask her to pick a dress from the *Vogue Pattern Book*. Then, style in hand, the woman would pose on a low podium in the middle of the room. My mother would study each woman's figure. She would walk slowly around her with the measuring tape, stopping every few inches to record a measurement, until she had completed a full circle. In the days before the "360-degree surround-view camera," this was how it was done.

Later, after the last client had gone home, we would talk about how to create the right fit for each woman. She taught me how to hand-sew a dress, about quality fabrics and fixings. My mother had an astonishingly good eye for someone who never had formal training, and she shared her secrets with me. She pointed out that a woman might have broad shoulders or a wider bottom, and would ask me to draw a pattern factoring in adjustments, such as shoulder pads or a shape skirt, to create the visual balance that would translate the essential style of the dress to that particular woman's shape. It was my first introduction to the concept of proportion that I would later study in more detail in art classes.

I found myself engrossed in drawing the patterns and as transfixed as my mother was by the transformations our efforts created. We could see how thrilled each woman was when she saw herself in her new dress for the first time. She would walk into the shop looking stern and careworn. We watched as the world-weariness disappeared and a joyful person emerged in front of our eyes. Laughing and twirling in front of the mirror, she radiated with delight. It was her movie-star moment in an otherwise drab day. There is an unmistakable look of confidence that blushes over a woman's face when she feels beautiful. It is contagious—a form of magic, a form of love.

My mother began to bring her hairstylist to the shop to consult with clients, expanding her services to offer complete looks for special occasions. Weddings were no longer the all-night elaborate celebrations they had once been. But even with strict government edicts closing parties down early, brides still wanted to look their best for their special day. The hours my mother spent at work mounted. Twelve-hour days were common.

Her only day off was Sunday, and that's when she went to the beauty parlor. Everyone worked six days a week, so Sunday was the only day working people had for that sort of self-care. It was the hair salon's busiest day, of course. My mother would take me with her. I loved this precious time together away from the shop and our everyday routine. I would watch the hairstylist sculpt and spray hair (the style had to hold for a few days). Sometimes the manicurist would paint my nails. When my mother walked into the salon, her entrance always caused a commotion. Everyone knew who she was and wanted to catch her eye or have a conversation. My mother's clients clustered around her in between their beauty appointments. Even there, on her one day off, my mother would still be dispensing beauty and fashion advice from under the hair dryer.

"You work all the time," I would say to her, my constant refrain. Sometimes it was a whine. "Aren't you tired? Don't you need more rest?" I wanted more of her attention. Even though I was with her in the shop, I never felt that she really looked at me. Her clients were her focus.

"We have to pay the bills; we have to eat," she would reply, as if this should be completely obvious. Of course I could see that we were making do with less. Of course I knew our survival depended on her work. Somehow, it didn't seem like the only thing that drove her.

"I love what I do," she eventually admitted. "I love my work. I love my clients."

## Passion Builds as You Succeed

I carried this conversation with me across time. My mother's eyes sparkled when she talked about her work. It seemed as if she was most alive when she was in the shop among the fabrics, talking with her clients, her seamstresses flitting around her and the machines whirring. Her presence was electric. Watching her showed me what it is to live vibrantly in your life's purpose—and the impact doing this has on yourself and also on others. When you show up at your best and give it your all, the passion you bring to your work invites in success. Success then fuels your passion, ever laddering up. The more success you have, the more your passion kindles until it's a fire that can't be extinguished. That is how it happened for me.

When I started my business, I emulated the care and the respect my mother gave to her community of clients as well as the workers and the suppliers. To this day there is never a moment in which I stop thinking about my clients. I always try to put myself in their shoes. I like to study a situation from different angles and think about how other people want to be treated. What are their expectations? What can I do, what can I create, to fulfill their needs and make their lives better? No matter what business you are in—cosmetics, tailoring, public relations, computer programming—when you keep your focus on your shoppers, your business will thrive.

When my customers look in the mirror after getting a brow service or using my products, I want them to experience that same thrill and see that same blush of confidence come over their faces that I witnessed on my mother's clients. I want them to laugh, to twirl, and to be beautiful. I want them to feel that magic.

I finally understood the meaning of that long-ago conversation. It was the *work* that kept my mother going. It fed her soul as much or even more than it gave her the ability to feed our bodies.

I realized that, at the end of the day, work, life, and business success *is all about love*. When you master your craft and give your expert gifts to someone else with love and care, you get love back. It's circular. Bountiful. It grows exponentially as you give it more energy and focus. This circle of love is what drove my mother to work harder. It would propel me in the same way, in days to come. The more you give, the more you receive. I believe this is a magic formula. The idea lifts you above difficult circumstances you may find yourself in. My mother's work created a sphere of light and love around us that seemed to hold us safe in a dark time and harsh place.

My own work would have the same meaning for me and the same effect on my family. I am not saying this is the only way to work, or this must be your way, but it is the way I found fulfillment, creativity, community, and success.

Years later, I would come home after my own twelve-hour day and my daughter would say to me, "You work all the time. Aren't you tired? Don't you want to rest?"

"I love what I do. I love my work. I love my clients," I would answer.

When you love what you do, work transforms into a passion. It is your opportunity to shine, and in doing so, you illuminate the lives of those around you. My philosophy on work and life revolves around the Four G's: Grit, Grace, Generosity, and Gratitude—key elements of a fulfilling existence. Something incredible happens when you give to others. And that is what I see my work as— giving my customers a respite from their day, a bit of magic just for themselves, and a new sense of their own glamour. At the end of every service, I hand my client a mirror and love to see their reaction. Beauty knows no boundaries; every one of my clients holds a special place in my heart. When you feel beautiful, you also feel powerful, and I take great joy in helping my clients look and feel their absolute best.

## Trust Your Intuition

I was busy at my mother's shop every evening but still going to school during the day. I was also preoccupied with trying to become my own person. Education in Communist Romania was a priority. The government wanted our youthful energies focused on learning skills productive for the state. I was sent to a school where I spent five years studying technical design, a combination of art and engineering. We learned how to design all sorts of products for mass production, even an industrial faucet. In art class, I learned about the golden ratio: the scientific formula for beauty and balance that we see all around us in art, nature, and architecture. I was fascinated by how art and science could be melded together into practical applications. This technical training has always stayed with me.

As students, we were required to wear a uniform to school. Ours consisted of a black pinafore and a blue top that had long sleeves buttoned at the wrists. I hated that this uniform made us look shapeless and the same as each other. Of course, being my mother's daughter, I loved fashion and the endless transformations it made possible. Wearing the same outfit as everyone else felt like an affront to the artist and free spirit in me that longed to express myself. I had to *do* something. Every day before school, I would hike the skirt above my knee in an effort to give myself some style.

I decided that I could no longer wear the ugly flat black shoes. One day, I brought my burgundy platform boots to school, hidden in my bag. I adored these boots. My mother had bought them for me when we still were able to purchase leather goods from Italy. I put them on and walked into my classroom, head held high, feeling very chic. It caused quite a stir. I liked the reaction!

"What are you doing?" my friend Leontina whispered to me. "You're going to get into trouble." I could see by the look on her expressive face that she liked the red boots. I could also see that she was afraid. The other students watched us.

"Why do we all have to be exactly alike?" I said back to her, loud enough for the whole class to hear.

No one answered.

It was a big question. It was *the* question that people were beginning to finally ask themselves privately but would not voice out loud. The whole culture itself had become a uniform—drab and colorless. No one could or would publicly question the rules. Something inside of me, the *me* inside of me, rebelled. By lunch, I heard whispers that the teachers were gathering. I knew it was only a matter of time.

The red boots were banned from school, but the sheer joy I felt by expressing my real self gave me a boost of confidence to follow my own path despite the naysayers. If I could do that in those circumstances, even for a short time, what else would I be able to do? It gave me a taste of what was possible.

This experience helped me to realize that we don't have to look like or be like anyone else, subscribe to a uniform way of thinking or even to a standardized image of beauty. Make changes to your look because *you* want to give expression to your inner vision of yourself—not because of anyone else. My grandfather taught me that our true compass is within. It powers our creativity, our resilience, and our aspirations. It speaks to us about who we really are, no matter what else is happening. Only one question remains: Will you allow yourself to listen to it?

I want you to hear that inner spark and let it breathe into your life and work the best version of yourself. Success begins with trusting your intuition and having confidence in who you are. I know that having confidence in myself and in my products made all the difference for me. Confidence is essential to being successful in this world. Stand straight with your head high. Move through your day on your own imaginary catwalk, with your own soundtrack playing. You have to tap into that inner confidence and positive mindset to make or do anything great.

## Turn the Life You Have into the Life You Want

At the outset, it's important to acknowledge that while many people are content with their lives, there are those of us who yearn for change. If you find yourself in that latter group, consider this: Transform the life you have into the life you desire. Your dream might be to become a pastry chef, to be a corporate lawyer, to write a book, to start your own company, or to be a present and nurturing parent. Whatever your dream is, I do not want you to let fear get in the way and hold you back.

You don't need to have all the answers, the perfect business plan, a prestigious degree, or a million-dollar marketing budget to start moving toward your goals. You need only to be yourself.

You can choose to create a fulfilling life. What you choose to focus on truly matters. Decide what you want for your life and how much energy you want to devote to each part of it: to work, to family, and to personal passions. You have agency and control over your own journey.

Taking action is essential. As the situation worsened in Romania, I began to understand that the life I was given was not the one I wanted. It would require planning, belief, and courage to carve out my own path. There is a person inside each of us waiting to burst forth and make a mark on the world. I know that you are one of them, regardless of your circumstances right now.

Your location does not define your identity. Challenge yourself to think beyond the confines of your circumstances. You can shape the life you desire, and you don't need to start with grand gestures; all you need to do is begin.

# The Mind Sculpt

Your mind is a muscle that can be trained. It doesn't matter what circumstances you find yourself in externally; you can build your inner resilience.

**Turn Up the Positivity Current**
Practice saying, "I can" and "I will."

**Take Action**
Do something today that moves you toward your goals.

**Break Out of the Negative Self-Talk Loop**
Change every "Why" that holds you back from taking action to a "Why not?"

**Trust Your Intuition**
This is your inner guidance system talking to you. Listen to it.

**Be Curious**
You never know what will bring your next opportunity.

**Gratitude**
Take a moment daily to be grateful for something you might take for granted: "*I have food to eat*," "*I am healthy*," "*I have people I love who love me in return*."

**Have Patience**
Dreams can come true if you don't give up.

**Believe in Yourself**
Remember this, when doubt arises. If Anastasia was able to succeed, you can too.

# CHAPTER TWO

# Always Have a Plan A and Plan B

**Welcome to Hollywood. What's your dream?**

—FROM THE MOVIE *PRETTY WOMAN*

The police interrogator sat directly in front of me. There was a small metal table between us. I could feel its cool, smooth surface under my fingers as I grasped the edges. I tried desperately to get my hands to stop shaking. The room was dark, almost pitch black. An old rusty lamp with a single bare bulb was the only object on the table. My mouth was so dry, but I was too afraid to ask for a glass of water. The officer clicked the lamp on and pointed the harsh white light at my face. It was exactly like a scene you might see in the movies, but it was all too real. Under the bright glare, he asked question after question in an effort to wear me down.

"Where is your husband?"

"I don't know."

"What are you hiding?"

"Nothing."

"Do you love Romania?"

"Yes."

"Did you know that your husband was going to defect?"

"No."

"Tell him that you want a divorce. He will have to come back here."

"No. I can't do that. I am Macedonian. In my culture, you cannot divorce your husband. You are married for life."

"Where is your husband?"

"I don't know."

"Your husband is a traitor. Your husband is a traitor!" He repeated this again and again.

The interrogator's words couldn't be further from the truth. My mind raced back to the day I met Victor Soare. I was walking with three of my girlfriends in a park that was a gathering place for young people in Constanţa.

"That's *Victor Soare!*" said one of my friends, pointing toward a man walking by us. She knew everything about him: He was *the* best bachelor around town, he had a great job, and a long line of women wanted to date him. More importantly, he didn't have a girlfriend. She smiled at him, trying to get his attention. The four of us sat down on a bench and gawked at him.

"Yeah, he's good-looking," I said. "Maybe I should date him!" Everyone giggled.

"There's no way he's going to look at you!" my friend said. "He's three years older than us and only dates very sophisticated girls."

"Are you kidding me?" I said. This was a challenge I had to accept. A wild idea popped into my head. "Let's bet one hundred lei I will get a date with him!"

"No way!" they all said. "You're on!"

I walked casually over to Victor, who was now standing beyond hearing distance of our group, and introduced myself. He was undeniably handsome. Tall, with piercing blue eyes that seemed to hold a thousand secrets, he had long, flowing brown hair that danced with the breeze.

I was utterly captivated. I felt a flutter of butterflies in my stomach, yet I knew I had to maintain my composure. As I stood there, lost in his gaze, a sense of certainty washed over me. I knew that he would be mine. I was destined to marry him.

"Hi, I'm Anastasia. Those girls on that bench over there are my friends. I bet them one hundred lei that we will go on a date. Do you want to make it half and half? I will give you fifty lei if you say yes, and I will pay for our drinks."

Victor burst out laughing. His face lit up; his smile was really so attractive. I continued to talk to him, trying to persuade him to do it. "You have to say yes, my friends are watching!" After more flirting back and forth, he eventually agreed.

"Let's go on a date. Saturday night at seven," he said.

"OK, I'll give you the whole one hundred lei," I said, feeling magnanimous because I had won the bet.

"I don't need the money," he said.

Later, he told me that he had really liked my confidence.

We went to an upscale bar that night. My three girlfriends came to witness our date, as they felt they played a part in it. I watched them as they sat at a nearby table, observing us. Victor didn't believe that they were there until I pointed them out. He laughed, clearly enjoying this crazy setup. I enjoyed it too. We were young, dressed up, and having fun. This lightness was such a rarity for all of us. After that night, Victor and I were almost inseparable. A year later, we were married.

But our future in Romania was bleak. Restrictions had tightened further; life had worsened. People had no heat against the winter frost and were told by the president to endure it by wearing all their clothes to bed. Even basic necessities were scarce, with shops empty. People did not have enough bread or milk to give to their children. The deprivations were never-ending.

I contemplated another option: leaving Romania. It was too dangerous to speak about it with others. It was almost too dangerous to even think about. There were harsh penalties leveled against anyone caught defecting, including prison. Victor's job, as the captain in command of a cargo ship, allowed him to sail to international ports. He had spent time in Houston and witnessed firsthand what it was like for people starting over in a new country. What it would be like for us if we left Romania.

"It is not easy to be an immigrant, Anastasia," he told me. "You will be far from your family, your friends, and from everything you know. You don't even speak the language."

His words did not sway me. It was true, I did not speak English, and I had no idea of the realities that were ahead of us. But I wanted to go. The suffering I saw in Romania, particularly for the children, was unbearable to me. I was young, strong, and just like when I first met Victor, I was willing to make a bet on us.

And so, we agreed. One day when he docked in Italy, Victor bravely walked off the ship and made his way to the American embassy and asked for political asylum to make a new home for us in America.

Now, in the police station, under the interrogator's relentless questioning, I did my best to hold on. I thought about my grandfather, who was like a rock standing strong against the thrashing of the waves, and his *komboloi* beads. "What is inside your mind and your heart is yours alone; no one has access," he had said. I remembered the girl who had worn the red boots to class who dared to dream something different. I thought of my mother and all the strong women in my family who had lived through war, poverty, and loss. I thought of my young daughter and the life I wished for her. The questions went on and on relentlessly. I was tired, cold, hungry. Still, there was something obstinate and strong deep inside of me that would not give in. A power that directed me. A little voice that whispered, *You can do this, Anastasia. There is something more ahead for you.* Maybe it was the destiny my mother bestowed on me when she named me Anastasia, which derives from Greek and means, "She who shall rise up again." Combined with Soare, which means "sun," I believed with all my soul in the brightness ahead of me that was just beyond the edge of this darkness.

After Victor defected, our whole family was under suspicion by the government. I was brought to the Constanţa police station many times. It was a stark concrete structure without beauty or soul. We had no rights as citizens, and police brutality was common. Every time I was taken to the station, I felt an almost indescribable terror. I did not know what would happen to me: Would I be hurt mentally? Physically? Would I even return home? I had no resources to defend myself other than my own courage. Sometimes I did not feel brave at all but instead felt intensely vulnerable. Sitting on a hard wooden chair behind a plain metal table for hours, not knowing the outcome, I felt fear wash over me. The only way I held on was by knowing that my mother, who always supported me, would quickly call her client, the wife of one of the officials. She would guarantee, at least, that I would leave the station alive.

We were living in a culture of secrecy and distrust. Our homes were raided without any notice by officers looking to see if we had any contraband from the West. They were also looking to confiscate any money or jewelry my mother and I may have received from her clients at the tailor shop. In Communist Romania, no one was supposed to profit. Of course, anything of that nature that we did have, we hid in deep holes under the frozen dirt outside of our houses. We were able to hold on to some of our family heirlooms this way. They eventually found their way to a new home in America, along with us.

## Life Is a Labyrinth, Not a Straight Line

It took almost three years until, through back channels, we were finally able to get the visas and passports to join Victor in America. Three years of putting my family under additional risk. Uncles, aunts, cousins who all thought we were crazy to leave our home. Yet my mother never wavered in her support for our plan to move to America. She was my backbone and could solve every problem. I knew that no matter what, even if I failed, she would always be behind me. She helped me carve out the time to build my skills for the future. At night, after we worked a long day in the tailor shop, my mother would make dinner and take care of Claudia so I could pursue my studies to be an esthetician. Victor had suggested that I do this because it was a profession that would not require a practitioner to speak English perfectly. I immersed myself in the scientific principles of skincare. I started to see the patterns (a skill I had learned earlier in my design school training) in the structure and geometry of the face. I watched women transform under my fingertips as I touched, soothed, and pampered their skin. The study and practice steadied me and gave me a focus as I went through the long bureaucratic process it would take to escape. The Romanian government required me to cover all additional expenses incurred by Victor's ship while in port until a replacement had been sent. The US embassy did a lengthy background and medical check, including blood tests, to determine if we qualified to enter the country. Even after I fulfilled all of these requirements, the Romanian government still would not issue our passports for two and a half years. Finally, I was able to take Claudia and go. But I had to leave my mother, my family, and everything I had behind.

## When you come from darkness, you appreciate the light.

## If you have light all the time, you don't know that darkness exists.

The Pan Am airliner touched down safely on the runway to the sound of applause from passengers. Everyone was ready to exit the cramped cabin after the nearly eleven-hour flight from Frankfurt. My own travels had started even earlier with a two-hour flight connecting from Bucharest to Germany. It was my first time on a plane. Soon we were walking through the hatch door and onto the white tile floors of LAX.

I could hardly believe I was finally in America! If I could have kissed the ground without holding up the flow of people behind me, I would have done it. I held Claudia in my arms, and we slowly made our way through the busy airport corridor. The terminal was alive with the noise and jostle of other travelers, colorful neon lights, and scents of strange new foods. I was not allowed to leave my country with any American money. I didn't even have one coin in my pocket to buy water or food. An onslaught of unfamiliar sights and sensations stilled me. The airport signs and directions were in English, which I struggled to interpret.

Finding my way to Customs and Immigration, I stood on a long line with other weary travelers. I was scared down to my bones: an overwhelming, visceral, sweat-inducing fear. What if we were rejected and sent back to Romania, after all that we had gone through to get here? Finally, after forty-five minutes or so, we were standing in front of a kiosk. A government official sat behind a tall glass window with a little door at the bottom that he slid open to receive documents. He was an elderly man in a gray uniform.

He looked at us not unkindly and said through the glass door, "Visa and passport, please." I looked over at the kiosks on my right and my left to watch what the other people on the lines were doing, and I handed our precious documents through the opening to him. The documents that cost me years of turmoil and worry, that represented all my hope for the future. He said something I couldn't understand. I wasn't sure if we had been cleared and accepted into the country or if we would be turned back until he picked up a large silver official seal and stamped the papers in several places with a loud thud each time, then handed the documents back to us. That was the best sound I'd ever heard. It was the sound of freedom! I walked beyond the kiosk to the next corridor. I was shaking all over with a relief that was so overwhelming I had to stop before I could make my way forward. As I stood against the wall of that brightly lit, shiny terminal, holding Claudia close, with a sea of people swirling around us, a feeling of complete joy rushed over me. Every fiber of my being tingled until I thought I would burst. It was a moment I will never forget.

I gathered us up to go the rest of the way. We had made it through Customs and Immigration, but my anxiety had returned. Frightening thoughts kept running through my mind: *What if my husband, Victor, wasn't there to meet us? What if his car broke down, what if he forgot that we were arriving today?* I didn't even have a quarter to make a call. My stomach churned; my heart raced. I was in a foreign country. I didn't speak the language, and I didn't know anyone. What had I been thinking to do this?

I followed other travelers to the baggage claim. Victor was miraculously standing at the bottom of the escalator, strong, solid, smiling. I saw him immediately. It was as if I saw Jesus! I felt so blessed. So grateful. Claudia and I would be OK! I finally exhaled.

It had been two and a half years since I had last seen Victor. He still was the roguishly handsome man that I had met in the park. He was dressed very casually and Californian. I immediately noticed that he was wearing blue jeans, synonymous worldwide with the fashion and freedom of Western culture. Blue jeans were contraband in Romania. Like many other things, such as coffee, cigarettes, and scotch, they were only available on the black market. Victor used to bring them back from his trips abroad. We felt like the best-dressed people in Romania wearing them. But mostly, we would exchange jeans for food. That's how it worked. People found ways around the restrictions; goods and luxuries were exchanged for necessities. We were lucky we had things to trade.

Now, at LAX near the baggage carousel, we happily embraced. Our plan was coming to fruition at long last! He had risked everything to escape. The embassy cleared his safe passage to America—to the place where we could build the future we wanted; where we could own a home and a business that wouldn't be taken away by anyone, as in Romania. He moved to Los Angeles for me because that was where I wanted to live.

When I saw Victor again, the tightness I held in my chest during the years we had been apart released its hard grip. We could begin our new life. A better life in the California that I glimpsed in those grainy smuggled copies of *Beverly Hills Cop* and *Pretty Woman*. I had the same aspiration as Julia Roberts when she declared to Richard Gere, "I want the fairy tale." Or at least I hoped for it.

Victor led us to the taxi he used for work, which was also his car, and we all climbed in. Claudia sat on my lap in the front seat. I could see she felt shy in a new place, around a man she hardly knew. I rolled down the window. The sunshine and warm air welcomed us. Palm trees greeted us. They lined the sides of the highway for most of our way. We drove for a long time, which I later learned was typical in LA. Finally, we stopped in front of an apartment complex in Sherman Oaks, a nice LA suburb. Victor walked around the car and opened the door for me. Together, arm in arm, we strolled up the path to our new home. I was filled with anticipation and hope. We were a family again. I didn't know then that this moment was the best it was going to be for us. It was July 29, 1989.

By September, the newness had faded, and reality set in. Everything was so different from Romania. There we had a big house with a big yard. Here, our two-bedroom modern apartment was rather sparse, small, and claustrophobic, with white spackled ceilings that reminded me of cottage cheese. Yet all around us there was abundance, from the lush plants and flowers that seemed to grow everywhere, to the fine clothes people wore, to the many, many colorful stores and boutiques selling all sorts of goods. I moved through the day in a sort of a dream state. It was as if I was living on another planet, or I was the heroine in a different movie. The supermarket felt like a luxury experience to me. For the first two weeks, Victor would drive me to the Hughes Supermarket (which later was acquired by Ralphs). I had never seen so much food in one place. In Romania, the shelves in the markets were all empty. Meat was a complete rarity. Mothers and children would huddle together on long lines for food, shivering, hoping for some potatoes or cooking oil or the occasional chicken if they were lucky, secretly praying for a miracle to grant them just a little extra something to take home that day.

Now I could push my cart up and down aisles that were filled to the brim with boxes, jars, and bins of food of every kind imaginable. I marveled at the incredible variety available in the stores that the other shoppers seemed to take for granted. I wished that I could wrap it all up and send it over to Romania to ease the misery and the hunger that I knew still existed there.

People who have gone through traumatic circumstances often experience survivor's guilt, and for a very long time I know that I felt this emotion. Somehow, I had survived. Even today, I can't stand to be under harsh artificial light. My first few years in America, I would start to sweat whenever I saw a police officer. Living through the interrogations marked me, changed my perspective. I came to realize later that it influenced my mindset as an entrepreneur. The experience of surviving mortal fear had burned away all other fears—fear of failure, fear of being wrong, fear of embarrassment. I found I was no longer afraid of those things. In business, I always think, *What is the worst that can really happen to you?* You might make a mistake, lose money, choose the wrong job for your skills. You can recover from any of this. You won't die. A problem is a challenge whose solution you have yet to figure out. I want you to think about that when you are afraid to go after a job, to express yourself in a meeting, or when circumstances feel against you. There is no reason to hide your shine from the world. Find that little voice inside of you, in your deepest heart, that says, *You can do this. There is something more ahead for you.*

Now in LA, I had so much. I pushed my cart along the supermarket aisles delighting in all the sights and aromas. I could buy all the chocolate bars I ever wanted, and I could eat them all too. My usually thin frame started to become rounder for the first time ever. I was driving to the store myself now, as Victor needed to work. I passed my driver's test even without learning English. Victor had given me the questionnaire that he had received because he thought everybody would get the same one. Of course, the test I was given was completely different. I panicked at first. But I am a visual thinker and had already driven in Romania, so I was able to understand enough to pass it on the first try.

With $200 that we had saved, we bought a gigantic old Ford station wagon with a hood that stayed open a little bit, a broken back window, and the exhaust hose coming out the side instead of the back. Unknown to me then, this car would be my steady companion for many years and would literally transport me to my future life. Victor put a Thomas Guide on my lap, which was a huge thick book with maps of LA (no GPS then). I started to attend English classes at a church several miles away in the valley that offered lessons to immigrants.

Yet even with so much abundance around me, I was inexplicably homesick. Inexplicably because it seemed that on a material level our plan was a success. We had been able to escape and get to where we wanted to be. Sometimes in pursuing what we want, we don't realize all that we actually have. In Romania the Communist regime was horrible, but I had love. I had family, my many cousins, uncles, my aunt. I had everything *but* freedom. Living in America wasn't like what I had thought and planned. I was alone, with only my husband and my child. I had freedom but not family, friends, or the support of a community. I realized that I needed freedom *and* family, that both were equally important, actually essential to my life. You can't always have everything you want; or perhaps not all at the same time. It was a hard lesson to learn.

That's when I started to glean that life is more like a labyrinth than a straight line. The path ahead is not always linear or clear; it may be hidden behind a curve in the road. I found that you need to have a plan A, and a plan B, and even after that, always be ready to pivot. Nothing is static; life vibrates and evolves with its own energy. In the song "Beautiful Boy," the famous Beatle John Lennon sang, "Life is what happens to you while you're busy making other plans." Staying open and flexible is key. We need to keep our eyes on the horizon and hold on until the future catches up to us. Challenges and obstacles will constantly show up, trying to deter us from that horizon we seek.

## Destiny Has Its Own Timeline

As a non-English-speaking immigrant in LA, the language barrier was one of my earliest challenges in my new life. It affected me more than I had expected. It was gut-wrenching to be unable to have a real conversation with the person ringing up my purchases at the cash register, or my neighbors in the apartment building, or other young mothers I met. I am a woman who loves to talk with other women. It is as necessary to me as air. In the culture I came from, entertaining was a big part of our lives. It didn't matter if you were rich or poor. A visitor to any of our homes was always greeted with a steaming cup of hot Turkish coffee or tea served in the best china or glassware we had, as well as some food—even if it was just a morsel. And then we would all settle in around the table for a good laugh, or cry, and share stories and advice on all aspects of life.

I missed conversations with my loud, close-knit family, as well as friends, people in school, or clients at my mother's shop. I missed my mother's infectious smile and her positive spirit. For the first time in my life, I experienced real loneliness. I wanted to go home. But we could not go back to Romania or Victor would be arrested.

Victor could no longer work as a ship's captain because the international shipping industry required proof of citizenship. Like many other immigrants, the best job available to him was as a taxicab driver. He worked long hours, taking on many extra shifts to earn and save as much money as possible. Victor tried to make the most of the work. I tried to conceal that I had been crying most of the day.

When I was alone in the apartment, sometimes the only adult sounds I heard were from the small TV set Victor had bought. One day, while folding laundry, I flipped through the channels and stumbled upon something called *The Oprah Winfrey Show*. It was a new phenomenon known as a daytime talk show. I watched, transfixed by this woman who was energetic, loud, and lively, much like my family at home. Her warm smile and hearty laugh felt like a big hug, reaching out to say, "You are not alone, Anastasia. There are other women just like you who are struggling with the same things."

Even though I couldn't fully understand all the words, I felt an undeniable connection to her. There was something about her voice that felt strangely familiar, yet I couldn't pinpoint its source. Back in Romania, we had watched bootleg copies of *The Color Purple*, and she looked entirely different in that film. When I began watching her show, I didn't immediately recognize her, but I was enveloped in a profound sense of comfort, as if her voice had transported me back to a cherished memory. That distinctive voice—warm, inviting, powerful—was like a soothing balm reminding me of the countless times I listened to it while watching the movie, sharing laughter and tears with those around me. Her presence made me feel anchored, as if I was surrounded by my family and friends and belonging to a narrative that stretched beyond just my own life experiences. It was a reminder of all the dreams and hopes I had while waiting to come to America, bridging my past to my present.

At the time we had the one TV, which was all we could afford. My husband, who spoke perfect English, would often watch the news or basketball. I made a deal with him: He could watch anything he wanted, except during Oprah's show. That hour was mine. Sometimes he'd want to watch something else and ask, "Why are you watching this? You don't understand what they're talking about." "I need to learn how she asks questions!" I replied. "One day, when I'm on her show, I'll know how to respond!" Never in my wildest imagination did I think I would be on her show. Somehow, I put that intention into the universe.

I made sure to be in front of the TV set whenever her show aired; it was how I perfected my English. Day after day, I listened to Oprah, her guests, and the women in the audience. With each episode, the English words became more comprehensible, and my heart slowly opened. Oprah was my guide and mentor, as she was for countless other women whose lives she touched without even knowing them. In 1986, Oprah had created Harpo Studios (her name spelled backward). Her show would go on to become the highest-rated talk show in television history. I still pinch myself that I actually got to meet her years later and call her my friend.

By late fall, we had Victor at home with us too. He had burned out, though we didn't call it that back then. Driving for so many hours every day on the freeways of LA was physically exhausting, but it was the loss of doing the work he loved that was hardest for him. He was highly educated and a trained navigator. He couldn't accept being unable to use the considerable skills and expertise that brought him such pride and success in the past.

He tried to find comfort in the books he enjoyed. When he could find the time between customers, he would park his taxi under some shady palm trees and read books on a variety of subjects from mathematics to philosophy. One day, when he was back in service after one of these breaks, a young man in an expensive suit and tie got into the back seat. Cabs did not have glass between driver and customer seats at that time.

The young man nudged Victor on the shoulder.

"Hey, someone left this book behind."

"Oh, that's mine," Victor said, reaching back to take the book. The young man started to laugh.

"Really? You read Nietzsche? A cabdriver reading Nietzsche, that's hilarious."

After battling for three years to get us here and then trying to rebuild some semblance of a good life, this was the last straw. Victor's anger boiled over and he got into a huge argument with the customer.

That was the end of that job. And the beginning of figuring out plan B.

## Resourcefulness Is a Life Skill

I cried until December and then the tears finally ran out. December is my birthday month. I was now a woman in my thirties. That birthday was, as Oprah would say, one of my "aha moments." Homesick as I was, I finally accepted the truth that we could not go back to Romania at this point. We could only go forward. I also realized that Victor was not going to rescue us. No one would rescue us. It was time to take my future into my own hands. I heard my mother's voice and my grandmother's hard-knock philosophy in my head: *Work hard. Don't complain. Figure it out.* With Victor at home to take care of Claudia, I began to venture out on my own. I needed to find work. But where to start?

People ask me, How did you figure it out? How did you find a job when you didn't speak the language well? How can I get ahead today in a slow economy? How can I stand out when everyone else seems more talented, beautiful, skilled? The world today is so overwhelming, how can I make a difference? How did you know what to do?

I believe that know-how and know-what come from digging deep within yourself to find your resourcefulness. Resourcefulness is an internal operating system to surviving and thriving. It can be the antidote to feeling stuck, hopeless, and not enough. By activating your resourcefulness, you make a mental shift from focusing on what you lack to focusing on possibility. We all have this problem-solving force within us if we choose to call upon it.

I discovered that shifting to a resourceful mindset made all the difference in dealing with obstacles and turning my vision into reality. Day by day, when I felt overwhelmed, anxious, or a resistance to moving forward, I would immediately say to myself three times: *You can figure it out.* I said this to myself until I believed it. I realized that when you firmly believe you can figure it out, you not only begin to see everything and everyone around you differently but you also find ways to make the most out of what you do have in order to get things done. Learning how to activate your resourcefulness is one of the most important skills you can cultivate to be successful. It helped me find the courage to take on changing circumstances and take action.

When I was operating in this problem-solving mindset, I generated an energy that made me more visible and vibrant, attracting new connections, ideas, and opportunities. I started to think about other immigrants in similar situations that would understand my challenges and possibly be able to help. With some trepidation, I reached out to Mihaela Corcoz, the wife of a taxi driver who had worked with Victor. It was a conversation that would change my life and put me on the path to my dreams.

We hadn't known each other well but had liked each other instantly. She was very pretty and wore her hair in a stylish French bob. Back in Bucharest she had been a flight attendant. Here she worked as a facialist at a salon in West Hollywood and had become very accomplished. When I called, she was eight months pregnant and looking for someone who was willing to cover her work during her three-month maternity leave with the understanding that the job would end upon her return. When I told her that I was an esthetician and that I would be happy taking a three-month job, she agreed to talk to her bosses about me the next day. It wasn't perfect, but it was a start.

Two days later, the phone rang. It was a beige rotary dial phone with a long winding cord that wrapped around me. Victor looked out from the living room.

It was Mihaela. "Anastasia, can you get to West Hollywood tomorrow morning at eight a.m.? The bosses want to meet you before the salon opens."

"Of course!" I always say yes.

"Go to the Giovanna-Jutta salon on Melrose Place," she said.

49

> **When you want something, all the universe conspires in helping you to achieve it.**
>
> —Paulo Coelho,
> *The Alchemist*

"Thank you, Mihaela. I will see you tomorrow!"

Melrose Place! I repeated the words over and over in my head: as I cooked dinner that night, as I put Claudia to bed, and when Victor and I turned on the record player and danced to Romanian music we both loved. Even after he was asleep, the words were a melody in my brain as I laid out the clothes I would wear. I could not sleep. My mind and body were tingling with the sense of possibility. My resourcefulness and daring had propelled me ahead in a great leap. Fate stepped in, in the form of Mihaela, to meet my effort. Tomorrow, I would go to Melrose Place in West Hollywood. I might not have my Julia Roberts moment on Rodeo Drive yet, but I would begin my journey toward it.

Everything conspired to bring me to this new start. By tapping into my resourcefulness, things started happening for me.

# The Resourcefulness Boost

Level up your creative ability to cope, survive, and thrive. Difficult situations and challenges arise whether you are a CEO or just starting out in life. You can boost your resourcefulness capabilities with these practices.

**Tap Into Your Problem-Solving Abilities**
Master doubts by telling yourself three times, "I can figure it out."

**Focus on Possibility**
When you look for solutions, they will find you. Make the most of what you do have instead of thinking about what you lack.

**Build Your Network**
Other people are willing to help; don't be afraid to ask.

**Take Action**
Forward motion creates momentum. Take one action today; the rest will follow more easily.

**Bridge the Gaps**
Choose progress over perfection. Don't let the need to do something perfectly stop you from doing something at all.

**Be Persistent, Consistent, and Open**
Don't stop if your first plan doesn't work. Pivot to a new plan instead. Remember, your destiny takes its own time to arrive.

# CHAPTER THREE

# Take the Stairs, Not the Elevator

**Nu sta ca-ti sta norocul.**
**Fortune falters when you stand still.**

—ROMANIAN PROVERB

The name *Melrose Place* was seared into American pop culture with the hit TV show about young people making their way in Los Angeles. Before that, in 1989, Melrose Place was just one of many streets in a chic West Hollywood shopping district. The street itself was lined with antique stores and boasted two salons, one of which was Giovanna-Jutta. The salon had opened a few years before. Its continental flair and cutting-edge skincare had been featured in the *Los Angeles Times*. Set slightly apart from the surrounding structures, the entrance had a tall glass door buttressed on either side by soaring windows of the same height. The elegance of the building seemed to invite you into a luxurious experience. A variety of upscale occupants have filled this remarkable space over the years.

On the morning of the interview, I made sure to park my rusty old car a few blocks away. I wanted to look like I belonged there.

I walked down the street, past all the storefronts with their beckoning window displays, to the building at 8471 and opened the heavy door.

I entered a dazzling new world.

Inside was an oasis of chrome and cleanliness bathed in the natural light from the huge windows. There was an immediate sense of calm and care. I was met by the owners, Giovanna Coffey and Jutta Mertens, who had already set up their stations in the front of the salon just behind the reception area. Giovanna and Jutta always arrived before all the others. Punctuality was a part of the salon culture, along with customer service.

They were a study in contrasts: dark and light, tall and short. Yet both were elegant, beautifully attired, and had the most perfect skin—which of course made sense because they were known for skincare and sold their own creams. Giovanna drew herself up to her willowy height, towering above me. She was very slender and had long dark hair. She wore a magnificent multicolored scarf around her neck. Jutta was petite, with short blonde hair. Giovanna had immigrated from Italy, Jutta from Germany. Both embodied what could only be called a European sophistication. Each one shook my hand. They were professionally cordial, although not overly warm. After our initial introductions and review of my background, Giovanna looked at me with her large brown eyes and in her melodic accent said, "So, Anastasia, what can you do for us?"

She was not being harsh. It was the way business was conducted at the time. Today's motivational approach to the workplace and drive for employee satisfaction was still decades away. Back then it was a simple transaction. You were there to work for the boss and to make their business a success. In return you were paid for your time and ingenuity. Giovanna and Jutta were in the early wave of female entrepreneurs whose futures were changed by the Equal Credit Opportunity Act of 1974 and Women's Business Ownership Act of 1988. Prior to those, it was nearly impossible for a woman to get a line of credit or even a credit card without a male relative to cosign for it. Giovanna and Jutta had broken new ground in many ways. This high-touch, high-stakes business was more than work for them, it was a calling and a vocation. They invested everything they had into it, including heart and soul. I was determined to learn from their experiences and, hopefully one day, to be like them.

## Say Yes to an Opportunity (Even if It Doesn't Seem Amazing at First)

I was interviewing for a temporary job that didn't seem particularly important to their business overall or to me. I viewed the job more as a necessity than a career opportunity. I did not see it as fulfilling any passion that I had. Yet there I was in front of the owners, two formidable women, being asked what I could do for them. I was keenly aware that there were likely others more qualified than me, even though this was just a temporary position. Despite feeling lukewarm about the job itself, I still needed to jump over hurdles to be hired.

What could I do for them? Me, a new immigrant on the edge of uncertainty with an out-of-work husband, a baby, and a broken-down car. A moment of doubt flickered inside of me. I was not like these two women, although I had a dawning desire that I

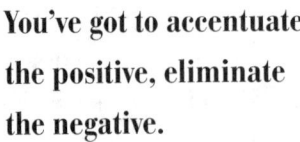

> **You've got to accentuate the positive, eliminate the negative.**
> —Harold Arlen and Johnny Mercer, songwriters

might want to be. My mind easily conjured up the many things I lacked that could disqualify me for this position. I was not sophisticated, highly skilled in this profession, English-speaking, or American. Maybe I was not good enough. Maybe I was not smart enough. None of that mattered! I needed this job, and I would not, *could not*, walk out of this salon without it. I had to figure out how to get it.

I took a breath to steady myself. I knew that I needed to focus on my positive traits and remember past triumphs to prevent a downward spiral of negativity. And so, I remembered. I remembered that I had successfully designed garments for the upper echelon of Romanian society in my mother's shop. I had worked with fashionable women before, just in a different way. I had overcome a lot of challenges to arrive at this turning point. The expertise and resilience I had gained through those experiences filled me with confidence. One thing that I could rely upon was that I had the ability to learn and to work hard.

"No one will work harder for you than me," I finally answered. I forced myself to stand upright to my full five-foot-three-inch height in front of Giovanna, and I looked boldly into her eyes. "Whatever the job requires or whatever you need, I will do it for you. I will come in early; I will stay late. Anything that I don't know now, I will learn quickly. I will make your clients happy."

My English wasn't perfect, what I said wasn't perfect, but I seemed to communicate something real and true—my commitment and dedication to work hard. Giovanna smiled at me for the first time. While Giovanna was styled and ready for the day, her lipstick, foundation, and eyeliner all expertly applied, Jutta wasn't wearing any makeup. I soon learned why. I was invited to give her a facial so they could see hands-on what I could do and to determine my skill level. They both remained silent throughout the service, offering me no clues about their assessments. The products they used were finer than those available to us in Romania. The delicate scents and the soft slip of the creams was so pleasing, I got lost in the applications. My nerves faded and time passed quickly. I realized that I could do this! In the end, I thought my results were good. Neither said anything. They asked me to sit in the reception area as they went to the back of the salon to consult with each other. My heart pounded. The salon was now noisy with employees arriving and getting ready for the day ahead. Mihaela entered. She winked as she glided by me, her rounded stomach gently protruding from her stylish maternity dress.

A little while later, Giovanna stood in front of me.

"We don't usually make a job offer on the spot like this, but you're hired!" she said. "Will you accept, Anastasia?" I was overwhelmed with relief, proud that I made the cut, and a little trepidatious.

"Yes, of course!" I said forcefully, wanting to show enthusiasm.

"When can you start?

"How about today?" I answered.

"OK!" She seemed pleased. "Welcome to Giovanna-Jutta!"

It is hard to start over. Everyone faces this challenge at some point; no one is immune. A corporate job ends, and you need to pivot. You finish school as a celebrated senior with straight A's but are now in an entry-level job. You are an immigrant and aren't able to do the same work you had done in your previous country—

like Victor or like myself. It might be a sudden change or one you planned, but you are now a beginner again.

Most of us find this uncomfortable. Many people are afraid to admit that they have something to learn. It doesn't feel Instagrammable. But no one starts out as the CEO. You have to take the stairs, not the elevator, to get to the top. It is the natural order. Working your way up is the best way to get to where you want to go, especially if you want to run a business. The captain of the ship needs to know how the engines work, what to do if they break down, and how to keep the ship running and moving forward. It is the same with a CEO. Successful careers and businesses are built by climbing up the stairs one step at a time: one hard-won accomplishment layered over the previous one. There are no shortcuts. If you try to take them, it is at your ultimate peril. On my first day at the salon, I was on the bottom step. It was my time to begin, to prove myself.

## Making Work Work

I worked alongside Mihaela at her station at the back of the salon for the last weeks before her maternity leave to learn basic salon procedures. Then, I was on my own. Getting the job was not easy and now I had an even bigger challenge—to figure out how to do it and succeed. I had to make the work work for me and for my family. Even though I had long hours at the salon and a lengthy commute, I still did all the household tasks to save money for the future. Every night I cooked dinner, cleaned the apartment, picked the toys up from the floor, mended and ironed clothing, and made food for the next day for Victor and Claudia.

All this was new to me. In Romania, I would cook for guests

because I loved to entertain, both then and now, but my mother made our daily meals. I learned to iron the fine garments my mother made for her clients as, in an atelier, this was the necessary last step for the final fashion look. Now that I needed to do this myself, I didn't think about it, or rail against it by saying "poor me." My family's values of *work hard, don't complain, figure it out* were deeply imprinted on me. I wanted to do it all very well.

I was lucky to have a lot of natural energy. I always had the desire to do better, to challenge myself to become the best I could be. I believe that old saying that anything worth doing is worth doing well. So when I learned to cook, I wanted to know how to do it well and then to continue to challenge myself to do it even better the next time until I became excellent at it. It was the same thing at the salon. I took so much pleasure in giving my clients the best facials and treatments, but I was still determined to figure out how to make the process and the experience even better the next time. Whether cooking, ironing clothes, or working as the CEO of a company, I believe there is always room for improvement.

Every day was an audacious balancing act, an act of courage, faith, and hope. This was a pattern that would go on for years. Some days I got it right; other days were messy. Some days, when I was tired, it was difficult to come home to find Victor on the couch, spiraling downward. I did my best to boost his spirits as I understood so well what it was like being in that small apartment all day. I think that all women, especially working mothers, feel caught up in this endless round of juggling everyone else's needs, wants, and desires as fast as you can without a moment to breathe, play, or imagine. Running yourself ragged and in high heels. Perhaps you are in this situation now. The dailyness of life, the grind, pushes up against your dreams. It is difficult to hold on to them or to stop them from disappearing altogether.

## The way to keep going is to keep going forward.

My way of holding on to the Anastasia who dreamed big dreams was to identify and invite joy into every day, if only for a moment. I called them joy bursts. It could be watching my daughter sleep; looking at the antiques displayed in the store window as I walked along Melrose Place, imagining them in my possible future home; making a real connection with a client; or learning something new. It's always possible to find little bursts of joy among the drudgery of everyday life, and it's vital too. These were the little ways I kept my mind on imagining a beautiful future and not on my immediate to-do list or what I could not have in the present.

## Show Up and Give It Your All

While I still dreamed of a more prosperous future, I was completely focused on doing the best I could at the job I had right now and on impressing Giovanna and Jutta. In order to do that, the first thing I had to do was get to work on time. Getting there was a great challenge in itself. Every morning, I drove my old car from Sherman Oaks to West Hollywood. It broke down frequently on nearly every curve along the one-lane road over Laurel Canyon, with drivers behind me honking and swearing. I learned how to drive on the freeways: a frightening maze of highly trafficked roads where gleaming new cars, limousines, taxis, buses, and trucks whizzed by at top speed. I also learned how to jump-start the car and how to kick it in just the right place to keep it working one day at a time.

Even with the many breakdowns and coping with the daily uncertainty that I would actually get to my destination on time, I didn't realize that the car was truly that bad until a client invited me to go out to lunch at a local restaurant called The Ivy. I usually ate my homemade food on the run between clients, so this was a special treat. When I arrived at the restaurant, the valet refused to park the car! The Ivy was not yet the super-trendy place that it became later, but the car was too much of an eyesore for their valet even then. This experience confirmed my decision to continue to park several streets away from the salon every day, so that no one who worked there could see it. The upshot was that I had to leave home extra early in the morning to allow for all contingencies, like breaking down, parking several streets away, and having enough time to walk to work.

And yet, despite these obstacles, I would still be the first person to arrive every morning with Giovanna and Jutta as they opened the salon. I kept my word to arrive early and leave late. It caught their attention.

They also seemed to notice many other things I did at work that just came naturally to me. Being helpful to colleagues and clients. Being resourceful: taking the initiative to find out information for myself. Presenting myself well. I believe in dressing your best whether it is at work, at a social gathering, or anyplace else.

> Believe in miracles,
> but don't rely on them.
> Work hard and make
> things happen.
>
> —Kris Jenner

Perhaps this is because I grew up in a more formal culture, or because my mother was a tailor. Whatever the reason, dressing well has always worked for me.

I made sure to dress stylishly every single day, and I still do. You don't have to wear the most expensive outfit or be the most on trend. There was a saying in the 1990s that you should "dress for the job you want." The idea being that if you aspire to upper management, you should adopt the image of someone who works in upper management. I think it depends on the profession—women in cosmetics, beauty, fashion, PR might dress more colorfully than those in a law firm. When I started out, I didn't have the option to purchase many different outfits, so I always wore a black skirt and a black or white shirt. I would add accessories: a scarf, high heels, a strand of large pearls (which were artificial, of course, but still fashionable). I spent extra effort styling my hair and applying my makeup. Over time, this became such a signature look that one day, to surprise me, all my employees at the Anastasia Beverly Hills salon showed up to work "dressed like Anastasia," wearing black, with high heels and pearls.

The most important thing I learned in those early days is that when times are toughest, that's when you double down on *you*. Remember who you are. Remember who you want to become. It is all about energy. Just as in the game of dominos, knocking over the first one creates the momentum. How you act, how you show up every day, creates the momentum—the energy, the luck—that propels you ahead. Throughout my life I've noticed that people with a strong work ethic succeed. This may seem obvious, and yet we are in a time when there is a renewed conversation about work, how we do it, what its value is. In my own experience, my dedication to work is what made the difference for me. I believe that success comes from having some talent, a bit of luck, but mostly it requires showing up, doing your best, and not giving up.

## Finding Your Jet Fuel

I did not think I was walking into my dream job or career when I accepted the temporary position at Giovanna-Jutta. But I found that the activity of the salon was a balm for my soul and battered heart after feeling so isolated, homesick, and housebound. The other stylists and skincare specialists welcomed me with their constant chatter. Giovanna and Jutta hovered around me throughout the day watching my work, offering feedback on my facial and waxing techniques. Now that I was a part of the team, their natural warmth and care extended to me too. It was uplifting to spend my days in the beautiful space. In this open, creative, collaborative atmosphere, I felt myself opening up. I began to understand that this was the kind of environment that I needed to survive and succeed, and an even more audacious thought welled up from that life spark deep within . . . the kind of environment I needed to be happy. Happiness is so much more of an American concept; most of the immigrants I knew and my family in Romania were focused on survival.

Much to my surprise I began to enjoy the work—the application of products, the conversations with clients about beauty and life, their delight in the results of the service. It was much like the joy I felt in my mother's shop when we watched clients twirl in their new clothes—when we could see that they felt suddenly beautiful, giddy, and free. This joy was jet fuel to me. I started to feel the work calling to me, rather than it being just a job I needed. I became so immersed in the process, involved with each person in my chair, that the days passed by quickly.

I wanted to learn everything I could from Giovanna and Jutta. I was mesmerized by them, how they treated the clients and staff. People didn't ask for mentorships back then. You learned experientially, on the job, through the work. I noticed that the early mornings or evenings, before clients arrived or after the last one departed, was when Giovanna and Jutta had the calm and quiet to focus on other aspects of the business besides customer care. I offered to clean their stations so that I could be closer to their orbit.

"You shouldn't do that, Anastasia," one of my well-meaning colleagues admonished me. "You are not a cleaning lady. You are an esthetician." She thought that cleaning work was below me, "not in my job description." That is a mistake that people make. If you do only what's in your job description, you will probably be doing that same job twenty years from now. Doing more gives you more in return. I think that employers want to see that you have the desire to learn and do your best. It is what I look for when I interview a candidate for a position in my company. A person may be qualified for a job and know how to do the tasks listed in the job description. That is good, but not enough. I want somebody who wants to do even more. I look for people who want to do better, those who are pushing the limits. It is necessary to put in the extra work and be willing to do all that it takes if you want to grow. I have learned that if you want to succeed, you have to do everything in your power to attract opportunity.

# You find opportunity when you put yourself in its path.

Those mornings and evenings were my living MBA. I listened to all their challenges with suppliers, keeping up with rents, competition, new methods, or products. I heard how they solved problems with vendors, clients, and even employees. I saw their grace under pressure—they never lost their temper, never raised their voices. I saw the care they gave clients, greeting each one at the reception area, and how they talked with them. They modeled elegance, business acumen, and a leadership style that I came to respect and wanted to emulate. Soon they noticed my interest, my attitude. If they had a special client scheduled at those hours, they would invite me to watch their facial and waxing techniques. Those were the services that I was doing at their salon at that time. Everything I learned from them I would apply to my own work as a facialist and a waxer. I improved. Clients were pleased. Giovanna and Jutta began to trust me with important clients. The more success I had, the more I wanted to do better. The better I did, the more success I had. The more I achieved, the more passionate I became about the work. I began to *love* the difference I could make to the client's skin and to their mood as well. My growing passion for the work fostered the inspiration to come.

After three months, Mihaela was welcomed back from maternity leave. One morning before the salon officially opened, Giovanna told me to gather up my supplies and to follow her. I went to get my things. I took a deep breath to steady myself against hearing bad news. Obviously, now that Mihaela was back, I was going to be let go. It was what we had planned from the beginning. I followed Giovanna until she stopped at a different station, closer to the front, which was a more prestigious location in the salon. Jutta stood there as well. They both smiled at me.

"This is your new spot, Anastasia," Giovanna said. "We want to offer you a permanent job here!" This time, I accepted the offer with all my heart. I was on my way.

# The Glow Seeker

How do you jump-start your career? Getting ahead when you are starting out takes determination. Use these success secrets for making your work work for you.

### Do More Than Your Job Description
Finding resources on your own, taking on helpful tasks, or volunteering for extra projects will fast-track you. Show up at 110 percent. Give every step your dedication, your brilliance, your full energy.

### Be Punctual, Reliable, and Present Yourself at Your Best
Being neat, clean, and professionally attired for your business makes a difference in how others see you and how you see yourself. Presenting yourself in a good light is one of the greatest tools you can use to achieve your goals. When you look your best, you feel your best. When you have confidence, you can do just about anything.

### Develop Your Skills
Immerse yourself in every aspect of your business and get the skills needed to level up. The more you know, the more you grow.

### Put Yourself in the Path of Opportunity
Don't hold back and wait to be discovered. Figure out how to put yourself in the path of mentors, bosses, teachers, and leaders to draw opportunity to you.

### Look for Joy Everywhere
Joy is the antidote to inertia and jet fuel for invention and innovation.

CHAPTER FOUR

# Master Your Craft, Success Will Follow

**Action is the foundational key to all success.**

—Pablo Picasso

The Giovanna-Jutta salon was becoming well known among Beverly Hills socialites, stylish business professionals, and Hollywood insiders. Melrose Place was a convenient location. My own reputation was growing too. Clients were beginning to ask for me. I would give them my entire attention, welcoming each one as a VIP. I always felt a tingle of excitement when someone sat in my chair for the first time and even more if they came to see me again. A repeat customer was the biggest compliment I could get. It was an acknowledgment of my craft. This feeling has never faded for me, even to this day, even after building a global company. My biggest joy is still when I go into my salon or work one-on-one with a client.

Every person had a story. Every face was an opportunity to try something new. I wanted to do my best so that person left the salon feeling cared for, cared about, and beautiful. Every day

69

I could see that I was becoming more skilled. I was becoming intrigued by brows in the interplay of facial features. When I had trained in Romania and had facials, my favorite esthetician, Mariana, would tweeze brows as part of the service. Facials in America did not include brows. In fact, the beauty and fashion industry did not put any particular emphasis on brows, nor did the everyday woman include grooming them in her daily makeup routine. Women going to the corporate workplace were becoming more conscious of their appearances, the culture was making room for new ideas. Pioneering makeup artist Kevyn Aucoin introduced his contouring techniques to the mainstream. Fashion-forward thinkers such as David Kibbe with *Metamorphosis* and Carole Jackson with *Color Me Beautiful*, as well as Steve DiAntonio who had helped to develop and expand the *Color Me Beautiful* business, offered new ways to build personal style based on color "seasons" and body types. I would join this creative explosion.

## Cindy Crawford, Michelle Pfeiffer, Faye Dunaway

One day, the most beautiful woman I had ever seen stood at the reception desk and asked for me. It was as if the heavens opened, and a golden spotlight was on her as she walked to my station tall, tan, statuesque. She was like an angel. Her long wavy brown hair framed her face before cascading below her shoulders. She had a small mole above her lip, a signature look that was uniquely hers.

"Hi, I'm Cindy," she said. She hugged me. The hug meant so much to me. She was so warm and friendly. Even without makeup on, everything about her seemed to glow. After a few pleasantries, she relaxed back into the chair with a sigh and gave herself to my care. I explained the different steps and products I would use.

I assessed her skin, the shape of her face. I thought to myself, *How could anyone be so beautiful?* She had thick brown eyebrows with high arches that defined her quintessentially glamorous but still girl-next-door look. They say you cannot improve upon perfection, but you can still give a diamond a little more sparkle.

"Thank you," she said. "I will come to see you again, Anastasia." She laughed and hugged me once again. After Cindy left the salon, Giovanna walked back to my station, smiling broadly, almost dancing with excitement.

"Do you know who that was?" she asked.

"No!" I responded. I really had no idea.

"That was Cindy Crawford! She was just on the cover of *New York* magazine. They called her 'The Face' of the 1990s!"

I hadn't even heard of *New York* magazine, but this was clearly important. The media had been so restricted in Romania, I had no real exposure to models or contemporary celebrities. I didn't know who they were. One of my repeat clients was a booking agent. I didn't know what a booking agent was either, but she was a lovely woman in her thirties, and over time we had wonderful conversations. Much later on, I found out that she had sent the models she worked with to me. I didn't think that much about it either, other than I was happy anyone was referred to me. I realized later that day that Cindy was a turning point moment for me. I was expanding into a new world.

After that, Naomi Campbell, Heidi Klum, Stephanie Seymour, Gail Elliott, Talisa Soto, and other models would come to the salon and ask for me. They were hardworking young women on the rise—not yet the supermodels they would become. A gorgeous porcelain-skinned actress making her way in Hollywood named Michelle Pfeiffer also sat in my chair and became a regular client. Each was a striking beauty, like goddesses I had seen in books or paintings come to life, with her own singular look and style that would make her legendary. I was enchanted and transfixed. Could women this beautiful exist? In public, each one seemed to live a carefree, glamorous life, but in private had to summon up the enormous discipline and stamina their work required—early mornings, late nights, long hours. You need a strong sense of self to overcome the pressures in their business. They made many personal sacrifices to master their craft. Nothing was easy, even if it seemed so in a magazine or on social media. There were no shortcuts. I respected their determination to go after their dreams. They trusted me with their beauty and, at times, bits of their lives. I am like a vault, or like Las Vegas: Anything said to me in my chair stays with me forever. In the beauty service business, confidentiality is key. I saw my service as being a little respite and haven for them—and I know that they appreciated the care I wrapped around them like one of Cindy's hugs.

I didn't recognize many of the models and actresses who walked through the salon door, but I remember vividly when actress Faye Dunaway stood in front of me. I immediately knew who she was: I had seen a grainy version of the movie *Chinatown* in Romania. I turned to jelly inside! She was the first international movie star I ever met. Well, the first one I actually recognized from the movies. As she sat down in my chair, I became unusually nervous and tongue-tied. Faye was used to the effect her fame had on others. She graciously put me at ease. She laughed—her throaty laugh known to moviegoers everywhere. It broke the ice. I smiled back at her and then settled in to do my work.

## Unleashing Your Greatness

Even as I did facials and waxing, my mind was churning. An obsession was forming. As my client base grew, my attention became focused on their brows. They were all different—thin, round, wiry, full. I was captivated by how shaping them, sometimes even by the tiniest fraction of an inch, could enhance my client's appearance. I became fixated, trying to figure out a unified approach to my work instead of creating a bespoke brow shape each and every time. All of my inspirations, and later inventions, have come from trying to solve problems for my clients. I needed to solve this one. I could barely think of anything else.

My mind was in overdrive. When I was sitting in traffic on my way to and from work, and in the quiet of the night when everyone else was asleep, I searched for the answer I needed. Something important was hovering around me that was just out of sight. I thought about what I learned in the past. First my uncle, the carpenter, came to mind, his ability to shape a straight piece of wood into rounded forms of animals or symbols. *Something straight could be made to bend.* My mother's teaching on styling dress patterns that balanced a woman's proportions to create a more harmonious silhouette. *Balance and proportion.* My design school training in the geometry of structural design and in classical art. I could see that brows were an architectural component to the surface structure of the face. *Geometry and structure.*

# Beauty is about balance and proportion, not perfection.

On Mondays when the salon was closed, I would do research at the Sherman Oaks library, which was near my apartment. I loved being surrounded by books; it reminded me of my student days. I would bring Claudia with me and sit at one of the many tables they had set up for readers. I would give my long reading list to the librarian at the front kiosk when I arrived. She would kindly drop the stack of books on the table so that I didn't have to leave Claudia even for a second. Books on design, architecture, art, the history of beauty and cosmetics—I read them all.

And then, with a jolt, I remembered learning about the scientific principle of the golden ratio years before in art class. The golden ratio is the mathematical formula that creates perfect proportion and balance. The human eye is encoded with the ability to recognize the harmony created by the geometry of the golden ratio as pleasing. We can see it everywhere around us in nature, art, architecture, in people when we perceive something or someone as beautiful.

I began to read everything I could find about it. The first known mention of the golden ratio is from around 300 BCE in Euclid's *Elements*, the Classical Greek work on mathematics and geometry. Known as the divine proportion, the golden ratio has been employed by artists and architects throughout the centuries. Leonardo da Vinci, Michelangelo, and Raphael all used this mathematical formula in their paintings. Art experts have said that one of the most beautiful faces in the history of art, the *Mona Lisa*, was painted utilizing the principles of the golden ratio. Five hundred years after she was created by Leonardo da Vinci, her allure still intrigues us all.

I remembered my art teacher, Asciu, talking about how important brows are in portraiture. If you wanted to change the emotion on the face, change the eyebrow. It came to me in a great whoosh of recognition—this was the answer! Even for myself. I

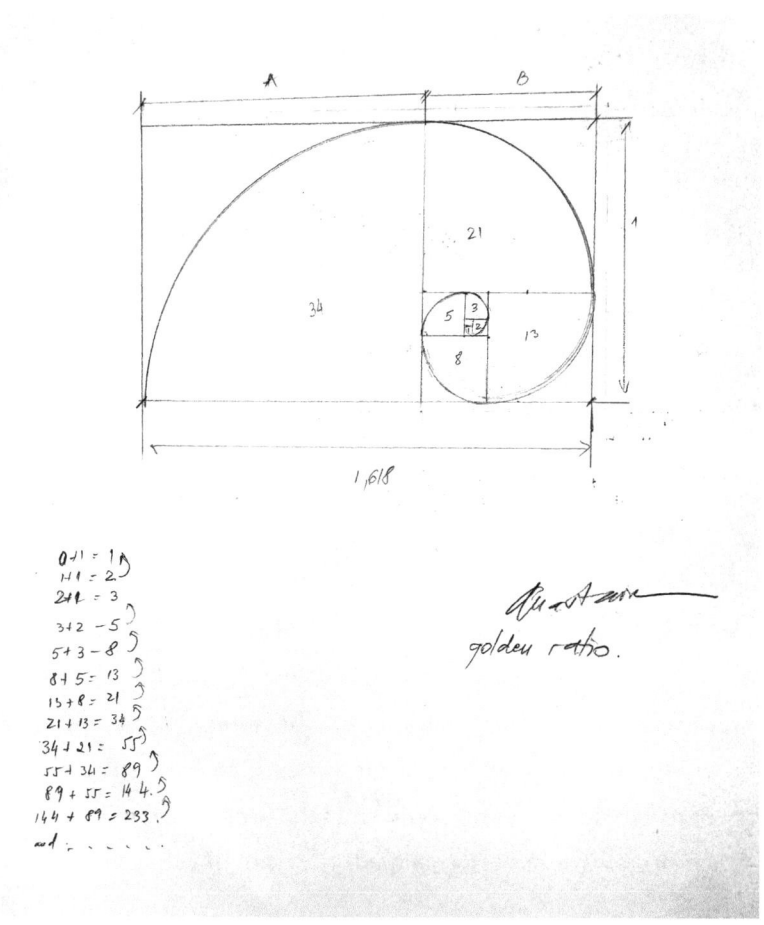

had very few photos of myself from Romania, as you had to pay a photo studio for one. Personal cameras were too expensive to own. In America, after we bought our first camera and I started to see a variety of pictures of myself, I thought: *Why is it that I always look so surprised?* In the 1980s, the eyebrow fashion was very thin and round, and my facialist in Romania had over-tweezed my natural brows into such thin crescents that they would never grow full again. Now I had a big aha. I realized that the surprised look on my face was actually the expression created by this eyebrow shape.

## The human eye is naturally trained to seek out balance. The golden ratio is nature's response to our desire for equilibrium.

Eyebrows are our most powerfully defining feature. Brows communicate emotions, and incorrectly shaped brows can leave someone looking perpetually surprised (like me), or confused, or even angry. Alterations to their shape drastically change the perception of the face's shape and harmony. By shaping the brows—making something straight bend, changing the geometry of the structure—you could shift the proportion and balance. When brows are expertly shaped, they tie all other features together.

## Excellence Is Not a Four-Letter Word

Now that I was reminded of the principles of the golden ratio, it was all I could think about. If I could figure out how to apply this scientific principle to reshape my own over-tweezed brows, I could provide even more extraordinary results for my clients. I needed to take this artist technique from the canvas and bring it to the real world. Every morning as I applied my makeup, I would work to reshape my brows—the length, the height—until I figured out how to get the proportions suggested by the golden ratio. I brought the tip of my arch down a little and lengthened the edge of the arch to come in line with the edge of my eye so it looked more natural. Before, it was too short and surprised. I'd figured out the right shape for my face, and now it was time to find the right product to help draw it in. The results I could achieve by using the eyeliner pencils available looked dark and defined. I wished I had something else to fill in the sparse hairs that would look more natural.

I searched cosmetic as well as art supply stores, but there was nothing, and I realized that I would have to create it myself. I began to experiment, mixing Vaseline, aloe vera, and eye shadow to create what we now call a pomade. Using a tiny, hard-bristled brush I found at the art supply store, I discovered I could delicately apply the pomade onto and around my brows in hairlike strokes. After many, many attempts, I found the right way to apply the golden ratio formula to bring balance to my own features. I was happy with the results. My clients and coworkers began to notice a change in my appearance.

"You look so rested today. You look so lovely," my clients would say.

"Actually, it is my eyebrows," I would respond, and then I learned to add on, "May I do this for you?" The response was always positive.

As more and more clients wanted me to shape their brows, I experienced such a joy burst. I was creating something new. I was making a difference! My intuition told me that I was on the right path, but I still needed to get better. I *knew* it could be better—much in the way a skier jumps their first mogul without falling or a cook bakes their first layer cake. Passion builds as you succeed. As you achieve, the desire for excellence grows stronger. This little bit of success got me hooked. I was all in and determined to do this work at the highest level possible.

I told Giovanna and Jutta that I wanted to add brow shaping to every one of my facials, gratis, as part of the service. I wasn't sure how they would react, but they did not object. Their only requirement was to keep up salon efficiencies. I had to figure out how to complete the brow shaping as well as the full facial or other service in the same one hour I had for each client. The other estheticians thought I was crazy to do this and work that much harder. I didn't care. Something inside of me was switched to the "all systems go" position. I was learning and moving forward. The only drawback was that the hourly schedule didn't allow me enough time per person to perfect the techniques for their face. Every brow was different, and I had to figure out its ideal golden-ratio-fitting shape each time depending on the person's features and dimensions. I knew that in order to get my application down from thirty, to twenty, to the ten minutes per person that was the optimum application time, I would need to figure out a method that would be replicable and efficient. And to create that method,

I would need a bigger sampling of women besides those who came to the salon. But how?

The only other times I had to do this were my days off from the salon, Sunday and Monday. I would have to use those days for this work. I decided to reach out to women at our church, the library, and the language school, offering a free brow service for anyone who wanted to try it. On those days away from the salon, I was able to take the time I needed to discover what was universally applicable, and started to codify a methodology that was not only quicker but repeatable. A happy customer is the best advertising. One woman would recommend me to another. My days at the salon were fully booked with hourly appointments, as was my time on Sunday and Monday. I didn't know where this was going, but I knew that I *had* to do this. I listened to my intuition, and I trusted in my vision. To perfect the system, I worked seven days a week for three years. I was able to get the method and the application time down to ten minutes. This eureka moment, the moment I developed the golden ratio method for eyebrows, changed my life forever.

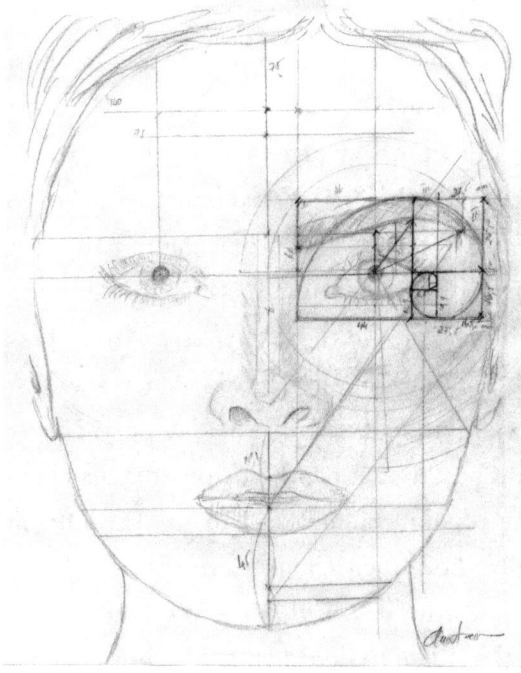

Directly above
the center
of the nostril

Center of the tip of
the nose through
the center of the iris

**BEGINNING**
I

**ARCH**
III

Bottom outside
corner of the
nostril with the
outside corner
of the eye

**END**
II

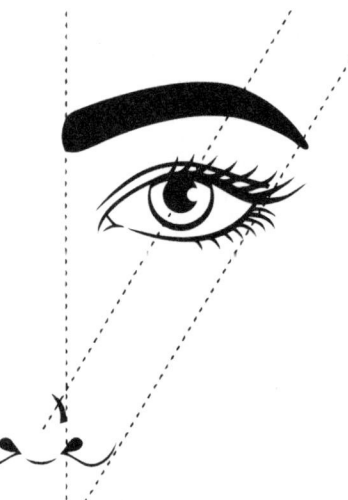

# The Golden Ratio

## The Art of Eyebrow Shaping: Science Meets Artistry

The journey to creating my eyebrow shaping technique using the golden ratio blends art, mathematics, and beauty. By combining mathematical principles with artistic vision, I created a unique method that celebrates individual beauty while maintaining harmony and balance.

### Understanding the Golden Ratio

The golden ratio, often represented by the Greek letter phi ($\phi$), is approximately 1.618. It is a mathematical ratio that appears frequently in nature, art, and architecture, and is believed to create aesthetically pleasing proportions.

### Anastasia Beverly Hills (ABH) Golden Ratio Shaping Technique

The most flattering eyebrow shape is tailored to the individual's bone structure. The ideal eyebrow shape should follow certain proportions, such as the distance between the inner corner of the eye and the start of the eyebrow, the arch position, and the length of the tail. The ABH Golden Ratio Shaping Technique relies on three measurements: (1) Brows should begin directly above the middle of your nostrils, (2) brows should end where the corner of the nostril connects with the outer corner of the eye, and (3) the highest point of the arch should connect the middle of the tip of the nose with the middle of the iris.

### Embracing Your Natural Brow Shape

One of the key principles of this technique is embracing the natural brow shape. Instead of forcing a specific shape onto the eyebrows, the focus is on enhancing what is already there. This approach ensures that the eyebrows are in sync with the rest of the facial features, resulting in a natural and flattering appearance.

### The Power of Makeup

While still adhering to the natural arch and thickness of the eyebrows, you can get creative with styling or with product application. Just like an artist uses different shades of a pencil to create depth and dimension in a portrait, you can utilize the power of makeup to shape and define eyebrows. Through careful application and blending, darker shades are used to minimize certain features, while lighter shades are used to enhance and highlight. Techniques such as eyebrow filling can further enhance the overall shape and look of the eyebrows.

### Creating Perfect Harmony

By understanding your bone structure and natural brow shape, an individual or makeup artists can tailor the eyebrow to enhance facial features. When eyebrows are shaped with the ABH Golden Ratio Shaping Technique and makeup artistry, they help frame the eyes, lift the face, create a more symmetrical appearance, and bring ultimate balance and the illusion of perfect harmony to your unique features.

## Don't Let Anything Steal Your Focus

The origin of the word *inspiration* is from the Latin *inspirare*, which means "to breathe or blow into." The muse breathes a passion into you, but that is not enough. An idea is just an idea until you do something with it. A passion is not a business until you build one around it. I didn't just stop at finding balance in my own brows, I tested my shaping on hundreds of women until I developed what would become the ABH Golden Ratio Shaping Technique, which creates the aesthetic harmony we crave, perfectly framing the unique face of each individual.

I know that there can be a dark side preventing each of us from chasing our light: fear of failure, fear of judgment, or even fear that you don't deserve success. People turn away from their passion and true calling because they are easily distracted by entertainments or the boring to-dos of daily life. It is important to fight against the power of the distractions and try to keep focus on what matters most to you. Keep mastering your craft.

Success happens by getting into the mindset of doing. It is like a tool that you constantly sharpen. The important thing is not to lose your focus and to continue to develop the skills and behaviors needed to attain your dream. I would do this by acknowledging what I felt in the present: "I'm overwhelmed, I'm angry at my situation, I'd rather watch TV," and then coach myself back to my path by taking action. We can walk into our bigger why by telling ourselves, "Yes, I feel bad,

> " If God gives you something you can do, why in God's name wouldn't you do it?
>
> —Stephen King "

83

sad, mad, tired today, but I am going to do something anyway. I will do one more thing today to master my craft." We all have days when we're sick, exhausted, or take our eye off the ball. But the trick is to be consistent and persistent, and not let those days turn into weeks. I have learned the truth that every entrepreneur, leader, expert, or master craftsman knows:

## You can't give 25 percent and expect a 100 percent reward in return.

The mathematics of success doesn't work that way. It is the sum total of effort given, energy expended, and expertise honed. Passion is energy focused on action. How you use this energy changes the trajectory of your life. When you immerse yourself in the doing, something surprising occurs. Your path becomes clearer to you through every misstep and with every success. The momentum you create keeps you moving ahead over obstacles both internal and external. You become *unstoppable*.

After years of experimenting, I produced a replicable template. Now I had a proven technique based on hundreds of brows. I had the knowledge that this technique turned ordinary to extraordinary. I had the confidence that comes from mastery and expertise. I believed with all my heart that brows could be my full-time work. The only question was, could I make other people believe it too?

# The Success Essentials

## Turn Your Passion into Action

Whatever you want to be, whether it is a musician, artist, or CEO, you need to turn your passion into action to achieve success. An idea is not a business until you build it. A song cannot be shared with the world unless you write it. When you use these tools, immerse yourself in your work, and dedicate ample time and focus to master your craft, you become unstoppable.

**Do Your Homework**
Learn everything you can about an industry, a business, an organization, your craft. Knowledge of the past and the present is the foundation for future innovation.

**Make Room for the Muse**
Inspiration comes in unexpected ways and places. Stay open and ready.

**Keep Your Eye on Your Bigger Why**
Do everything in your life with that in mind.

**Don't Be Derailed by Fear**
Don't waste energy on distractions or detractors. Use all your resources to keep moving forward.

**Do Your Best**
Excellence is the outcome of doing little things well over time.

**Unleash Your Greatness**
Work it until it works. Success doesn't just happen. Your greatness is unleashed in the doing.

# CHAPTER FIVE

# Don't Take No for an Answer

**Just remember, you can do anything you set your mind to, but it takes action, perseverance, and facing your fears.**

—GILLIAN ANDERSON

Many people who think of themselves as artists don't believe they can be business leaders; many business leaders do not think of themselves as artists. For me, artistry and business are both creative endeavors that have melded together in synergy and harmony. Until this point in my life, I had been immersed in my artistry. Now, I had a growing sense of certainty that the art form of shaping brows I had created could become a stand-alone service in the salon business, not merely an add-on to a facial. I began to envision myself pivoting from being a general esthetician to a brow specialist, a profession that I would come to invent.

I hoped that I would be able to do this at the salon. I felt loyal to Giovanna and Jutta, as they had taken a chance on me when I needed it most. One day, in a quiet early morning, I asked them for a private conversation. I was nervous but I also believed that my golden ratio methodology was something unique and marketable.

We sat together in their little office. I began to make my "business case," as I would refer to it now. At that time, I just wanted to share my technique using the golden ratio, the value I thought it had, and the new position I wanted in the salon. The discussion did not take long.

"I have been including a brow service as part of my facials, as you know," I said. "My clients love it. Many tell me that they are coming back for facials every few weeks just to get their brows groomed. I believe that we could offer brow shaping on its own as a separate service. I would like to become the Giovanna-Jutta salon brow specialist."

They gave me their full attention, but neither Giovanna nor Jutta reacted immediately. I understood that they would need to absorb the idea. I knew they would always think through all the implications of requests, actions, and business items before responding. It was a skill that served them well to keep things calm and steady in the vibrant environment of the salon. It was one that I would come to adopt in the years ahead.

"How much do you think you could charge for a brow service only?" asked Giovanna, getting down to business.

"Ten dollars per service." I threw the number out to them. We talked about pricing for a little while and why I thought this new service would be embraced by existing clients and new ones. I hoped that my passion about it and my business logic would be convincing.

"We will think about it, Anastasia." The conversation concluded. It was the best I could ask of them.

I tried to be patient and go about my everyday work as if my hopes did not hang in the balance. I think that waiting for something to happen is actually so much more difficult than taking action. However, at this moment, waiting was the *only* course of action, so I waited with all my might. Several weeks passed. Finally, they gave me their answer. It was a firm "no." Their salon, their business, their own passions lay in skincare, and they believed that a separate brow service would be a distraction. Today we might say that they considered it not "on brand." I was crushed. I was disappointed that they could not see the opportunity that I could so clearly. How was I going to move past what felt like a huge rejection? Once Giovanna and Jutta made a decision, I knew I would not be able to change their minds. I had to accept that they needed to do what they thought was best for their business.

What do you do when you hit a wall? When your idea, project, program, or dream meets up against "no"? We all get to a "no" in our lives—sometimes this happens during our school days as we begin to imagine our future and certain paths seem unavailable to us, or it can be in a work environment when we don't get the opportunity or promotion we wanted. Over time, I have come to see these "nos" as part of life's compass setting and resetting our direction. They are little turning points, course corrections on our path. They test our resolve, our drive, our faith in ourselves. Sometimes a "no" is the universe saying to us, "Not now—you need to do or learn more." It can be an indication we need to bide our time and keep doing what we are doing to be ready for the next opportunity. These "nos" can also put us onto a different path, helping us to change direction or pivot. It is OK to alter your course if it is necessary for your growth. Most people zigzag their way to success. I think everything in life happens for a reason; we just need to listen between the spaces to hear what this "no" is telling us. After several weeks, I came to my radical conclusion.

# Even if an idea is not good for someone else's business, it doesn't mean it isn't good for yours.

Now I had a decision to make. I thought about it as I made dinner, as I cleaned the house. I thought about how comfortable I was in the salon—I had finally made some friends. I thought about the money I made that supported our family. The most practical thing to do, given our circumstances, would be to keep the job and let this dream go. But! The word landed on me with great big thud. But . . . a little piece of my heart was breaking. But . . . could I really be an esthetician for the rest of my life? Is this why I braved all the hardships to come to America? Is this why I scrimped and saved these past few years?

That night, as I got ready for bed, I looked in the mirror at my shaped brows. They no longer looked like thin, over-tweezed crescents above my eyes. I thought about my mother building her own tailoring business against all odds, and the long line of brave seekers and entrepreneurs in my family who paved the way for me. I could stay put and never answer the call of destiny, or I could take a gamble on myself.

The next day, I told Victor that I wanted to open my own

brow business. Making this decision was only the first hurdle; I
would encounter many more just
to get to the beginning. Victor was
worried about money. More importantly, he could not envision
what I was proposing. He was
held back by his limited beliefs

> **You don't choose
> your passions; your
> passions choose you.**
>
> —Jeff Bezos

about what was possible for immigrants such as ourselves and
still reeling from the loss of his own career. He thought it was
crazy. He thought *I* was crazy.

"How can you have a business?" he said. "You barely know
how to write a check. You barely speak English. You aren't American. There are American people born in this country who don't
open their own business."

"I have to try, Victor. We made such sacrifices to come here. I
need to prove myself. I have to do this. What do I have to lose?"

"You're an immigrant," he said even more strongly for emphasis, as if I wasn't aware of this fact, as if being an immigrant
was a barrier that could not be overcome. I could see that I was
pushing up against an unyielding resistance, a tightly closed steel
door. I felt differently than he did. All around us I saw the evi-
dence of what immigrants had been able to achieve in America. I
was proud to be in this group, not humbled. I still feel proud to
this day to be an immigrant.

"I don't care about those things," I said to him simply. "I will
figure it out. Victor, this country was built by immigrants."

We were at an impasse. Despite his reaction, I was not dis-
suaded. The very act of revealing what I most yearned for and
desired actually freed me. Something lit up inside. I felt fired up.

I had saved $5,000 through all my thrift, and I could put it toward my own business. I learned from Giovanna and Jutta that the right location played a huge part in contributing to business success. West Hollywood was good, but I still remembered what I had set my heart on when I had chosen to move to Los Angeles.

That Sunday, at breakfast, I opened the *Los Angeles Times* to the real estate listings in the back. "I am going to rent a room in a salon and do brows," I told Victor. "But it has to be in Beverly Hills."

## Believe in your dreams, even if others don't.

I still worked for Giovanna and Jutta as I got myself organized. Many people had come and gone at the salon over the past few years. I had learned from their example that it is more advantageous in the long run to never leave a job before getting set up for the next opportunity; I would not paint myself into a corner by making ultimatums, and I never let up on my professionalism. Instead, I went quietly about getting myself ready to make a move but still gave 110 percent to my clients and my bosses. I had watched for years how Giovanna and Jutta supported each other and benefited from having a partner. I decided to invite Mihaela to join me: I trusted her, and I trusted her work ethic.

"Let's open a business together!" I said to her when we had a break between clients. I could see in her eyes that she felt complimented by my asking her. I knew that we respected each other. She didn't have to think about it. She smiled at me but shook her head. "I can't. I have two kids now. I need the steady income. I am going to stay here, Anastasia." She knew what was right for her. I understood. It is hard to walk away from a steady income and leave behind what you know. It was even more difficult for a person like Mihaela who had already made such a big risk in moving from Bucharest to LA.

Could I really open a business for myself and do it by myself? I felt truly alone. I wished my mother, and my family, were closer to talk with me, to hold me, and to prop me up. The doubt passed. It was replaced by a sense of excitement. I *had* to do this. I was *supposed* to do this. I felt compelled to do it. I was willing to take the risk, to make the leap of faith, and it felt like the right time.

I continued to scan the real estate listings, and I finally found the perfect place around June 1992. The Juan Juan salon in Beverly Hills had a room available to rent. It was a small space, seven by nine feet, adjacent to the central hub of the salon. The room had no windows, but the location of the salon was just what I wanted. Situated at 9667 Wilshire Boulevard, it was on a street that was one of the major shopping destinations in Beverly Hills. Juan, the owner, was a genuinely warm, charming, and upbeat man who had come from Lebanon determined to build a thriving business. We had much in common, including our drive and the desire for success. He rented the room to me at $1,000 per month, a sum that would quickly eat up my savings. In addition to fronting the money on the rent, I would also have to buy a chair, a steamer, other equipment, and products. It would not be easy, but I felt that the proximity to his stylists, clients, and the upscale department stores—Saks, I. Magnin, and Neiman Marcus were all nearby—would help my business grow.

The day after I shook Juan's hand, agreeing to rent the room, I drove to the florist and bought the biggest arrangement in the store. I presented it to Giovanna and Jutta. It was a grand gesture and a humble thank-you. We went to their office to talk.

"I am going to open my brow studio," I told them. "I am taking a room at Juan Juan in Beverly Hills." They appeared surprised, but to this day, I am not sure if they actually were. "Thank you for the opportunity you gave me and for everything you taught me these past few years," I said, my voice shaking with the emotion I felt at this parting. "I learned so much from both of you. This is my two-week notice, but I will stay for as long as you want me to stay."

I believe in leaving a job with grace and professionalism. When I became a boss, I always appreciated the people who did this. Business, as in every other part of life, is about relationships. We carry them with us as we go forward. Elegant to the end, Giovanna and Jutta wished me well, kissed me on both cheeks in the European style, and let me leave at the end of the day, though I'm sure they didn't want clients to go with me.

## Confidence Is Currency

Many of my well-known clients did follow me to my new space, but I still had openings in my schedule. I would not be able to sustain the rent without a full roster of clients. Nonetheless, I was optimistic. I think it is my nature to always see the possible, to be the proverbial "glass half full, not half empty" person. Even more than optimism, I felt a confidence in myself based on the skills I had honed the past few years. Authentic confidence, felt deep in your bones and carried in your posture, head held high, comes from mastering your craft. It is currency. It is charismatic. I felt confident that people would want my brow service once they learned about it. I just had to get them to experience it.

I already had a proven method that made it easy for someone to try: By offering a free service, I intuitively knew I would overcome their hesitation. If a woman liked the results, which most did, she would not only come back again but also refer a friend. I was following in the footsteps of one of the industry's great innovators, Estée Lauder. In his book, *The Company I Keep*, Leonard A. Lauder—Estée Lauder's son and chairman emeritus of the Estée Lauder Companies Inc.—wrote, "A free sample was the basis on which Estée Lauder was built." People don't see the downside of something free. Of course, sampling now has become a great staple in the beauty business. We still do it at Anastasia Beverly Hills to this day.

My first outreach was inside the Juan Juan salon. My room was next to the food bar that Juan provided for his clients. I invited every person who ate there to try my service for free. I also invited every hairstylist, colorist, and shampoo lady in the salon to do the same. I did the same with employees and customers at the nearby salons too. I then walked down Wilshire Boulevard to the luxury department stores. At every cosmetic counter, I offered a free brow service to all the makeup artists and salespeople if they would send customers to me. When I was not working on clients, I was out talking to people about my work. If you truly believe in what you are doing, when you are working on your passion and purpose, it is easy to talk about it with other people. An entrepreneur has to put aside any sense of shyness or reserve. If you do get shy, you can practice what you want to say in a mirror before-hand to get comfortable; what you say will become better and more persuasive with practice.

That's how I met my friend Charlene Roxborough Konsker and eventually became the godmother to her daughter. I saw a stylish young woman walking down Wilshire Boulevard on one of my networking missions. She had the most beautiful curly blonde hair that was like a cascade of sunshine. Her movement, her energy drew me to her. I went up to her and told her that I liked her hair, then asked if I could offer her a free brow service. She was surprised, but we instantly connected, and she agreed to come to my salon on the spot. I shaped her brows, and a forever friend-ship formed. She had just graduated from college and worked at an upscale shoe boutique next door to Juan Juan. Later, she would do the styling for music videos, sending me her customers, friends, and people she worked with, who all became my steady clients.

It is always in the doing that success unfolds. Every day, I would wake up thinking about how I could generate new business. I had the idea that I needed to get at least one new client per day. Today, I still wake up every day thinking about how to generate new business. I still have the need to talk with women, to learn new things for them, and to keep creating things for them. I still need to get at least one new client every day. Each person always brings another along with them, say their mother, their sister, or their best friend.

It is a tried-and-true way of doing business. Advertising is important. Nowadays, social media is important. But nothing is more important or effective than word of mouth.

While my artistic focus was on a client's brows, I still did facials and body waxing. I learned from other facialists about Pevonia, a professional line of products for facials and body waxing used in spas and by estheticians. I would call customer service on the phone, give them my order, and

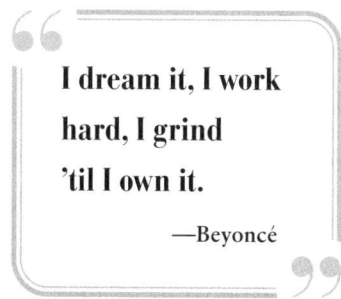

I dream it, I work hard, I grind 'til I own it.

—Beyoncé

then pay COD, cash on delivery, when the products arrived. One day, when I rang customer service, they told me that their new policy was to take credit card orders only. I didn't have a credit card or any idea where to apply for one. I asked one of my clients and she told me to go to Wells Fargo.

I went to the branch nearest my salon. I went up to the teller and asked how to apply for a credit card. The teller pointed to the nearby row of executive-style desks; one had a discreet sign on it that read Credit Manager. Behind that desk sat a man in his forties. He kindly invited me to sit down in the low, softly cushioned chair that faced him. He made no secret about looking me over. I could feel him evaluating me, taking in my self-imposed uniform of a black dress, heels, and pearls. He pulled a form out from one of his desk drawers and a pen that said Wells Fargo on the side of it.

"I would like to apply for a credit card," I said.

"Do you or your family own a home or have any other credit cards?" he asked.

"No," I said. "We are immigrants. I have only been in this country for five years. But I work very, very hard, seven days a week, and I have my own business."

His answer was disappointing. "I'm sorry but you don't qualify for a card. We can't issue a card if you don't have a credit history; we need some sort of collateral." I did not know business terminology. Seeing that I did not understand, he went on to tell me that they needed to know that I could pay the money back. They needed to know I could pay them, and I needed that credit card. I thought to myself, *What is it that I could do to turn this around?* He must have some leeway in his position to grant me a card. An idea floated into my head.

"I have money in my account," I said. "Give me five hundred dollars, and if I don't pay it back in time, you can take the money from my savings. If you give me this credit card now," I added, "I promise that I will be a Wells Fargo customer forever!" He smiled. I could see that he had warmed up to me.

I had done everything I could to persuade him short of getting down on my knees to beg. He finished the form in silence and then finally looked up. Our eyes met. I held his gaze. He nodded. I watched as he put my paperwork through. I kept the promise I made. My business account is with Wells Fargo to this day.

It was a miracle that helped my business grow. Within six months, I no longer had concerns about paying the rent. One year later, a bigger room became available at the salon. It had two large plate-glass windows that faced Wilshire Boulevard. I could afford to take it.

I continued to talk to anybody and everybody about my work and invite them to the salon. My fashion models (including Stephanie Seymour, Naomi Campbell, and Heidi Klum) and Hollywood stars had followed me to my new space from Giovanna-Jutta. Now many other celebrities and people in all aspects of the entertainment industry found their way to my chair. This industry buzz caused magazine editors to take notice. Magazines, the ultimate influencers of the day, were more focused on fashion than beauty. *Allure*, which had launched a few years earlier in 1991, changed that landscape, bringing beauty to the forefront. In the magazine, they showcased up-and-coming makeup artists and brands. Somehow, someone led them to me, and they wanted to do a small article. It was the huge opportunity I had been hoping for. However, there was a hitch. They would only include me if they could mention a celebrity client.

I had never asked a client something of this magnitude. I thought about who might be open to such a favor and also would not be upset at my asking, even if their answer was no. Michelle Pfeiffer immediately came to mind; she was such a genuine and generous person, beautiful outside and inside as well. I called Michelle and explained what the magazine wanted. Michelle was gracious, as always. She said that I could reveal that she was my client. I am grateful to this day to her for contributing to my first break. I also learned something important: Everyone liked talking about eyebrows. When I did someone's brows, there was always an immediate difference, an instant gratification. When a client walked down the street after an appointment, other people could see her shaped brows and wanted those results for themselves, which was my best advertisement. I was on the right path. The *Allure* story led to a bigger *Vogue* article about my eyebrow shaping that changed everything—suddenly, I was completely booked up doing brows. My vision of becoming a brow specialist, which I had shared with Giovanna and Jutta, was now a reality. Magic met me head-on.

I worked morning to night, seven days a week. My other waking hours were taken up with commuting and the daily housekeeping tasks of our family life. I felt energized by the work and also by being able to view the busy bustle of Wilshire Boulevard from my new room. Sometimes, as they walked by, my clients and friends—Shannon Hill, Bethenny Frankel, Mychelle Charters—would gently toss a few little street pebbles at the windows to greet me or, after-hours when the main salon had closed, to signal me to open the locked door and let them in. During this time, I had become friendly with the woman whose room was next to mine. I learned that her name was Yolanda and she was from Poland. No matter how early I came in or late I stayed, she was there. She never complained; instead, she was always pleasant to everyone in the salon.

One night after the salon closed, the manager, John Azar, a wonderful person who helped me a lot, and his stylists had a birthday party for her. Yolanda came to my room and invited me to join them. She offered me a slice of her birthday cake. It was November 16, 1996. I would never forget that date.

"We barely see each other," I said to her as I held the paper plate with a giant piece of whipped-cream-covered cake. "How many years have you been here?"

"I'm turning sixty today. I've been here for twenty years."

Her simple statement hit me hard. I felt rattled to my core. Yolanda had been working day and night in the same small room for twenty years! I couldn't imagine that for myself. Undeniably, I was filled with gratitude to have had the opportunity to focus on what I loved to do and to continue to master my craft. However, there was one thing I knew with complete certainty about my time at Juan Juan.

This was my starting point, not my destination.

That conversation was more than a wake-up call, it was a

shake-up call. I realized that it was time to take action once again. I would not allow myself to still be working in that small room when I turned sixty. While it seemed to be right for Yolanda, it would not be right for me. I believe each of us deserves to design the life that fulfills our own dreams. Lurking beneath the everyday to-dos, a grand idea had been percolating. The bold, breathtakingly audacious idea to open my own salon and perhaps even make my own line of professional products for eyebrows. I had been making little pots of my pomade mixture of Vaseline, aloe vera, and eye shadow in my kitchen to create a creamy pigmented product that could be applied in natural-looking hairlike strokes on clients' brows. But I was limited in the color and the quantity that I could produce. Clients would tell me that they looked great when they left the salon, but after a shower, the pomade came off. They wanted to have a supply of it in the interim between appointments. It was a problem that needed solving. What my clients needed, I was driven to provide.

## Invest in Yourself

I knew that in order to find the solution and to continue to grow, I would need to open myself up to the world outside of Juan Juan. I had learned from the makeup artists that the biggest international industry trade show, Cosmoprof Worldwide, took place annually in Bologna, Italy. Italy was where the best quality cosmetics were produced. If I wanted to find a possible manufacturer, that was where I needed to go. Closing my business for several days and buying airline tickets and hotel rooms would be big expenses.

I had taken a gamble on myself; now I needed to invest in myself as well.

I hesitated, like most women do. I believe that investing in ourselves, and in our deepest yearnings, is one of the biggest challenges that women face in business and in life. We tend to be the keepers of the practical. Dreams are elements of air, not of earth. They emerge from the intangible realms of yearnings, aspirations, and intuition. Yet often even before we begin to dream, that imagination-killer voice in our head whispers, *Who are you to spend money on yourself? Who are you to want more?*

It whispered to me too. I wrestled with it. The guilt, the self-judgment, the belief that there is a limited supply of money and it should be held very tightly. I had to learn to lean on my confidence in my craft. I had to remember who I was, what I had already done, and to believe that my skills were worth investing in—that I was worth investing in. *You* are worth investing in too.

I looked at the road stretching out in front of me. My yearnings and desires, my intuitions and dreams came into view. What kind of life did I want for myself? I also thought about my daughter and all that I wanted for her. Investing in my future would not only set the course of my life, but hers as well. I knew that I had to choose growth. I steeled myself to ignore the imagination killer in my head and told myself instead, "I will find a way. I will save until I can."

> If you can't fly, run. If you can't run, walk. If you can't walk, crawl, but by all means, keep moving.
>
> —Martin Luther King Jr.

You can do this too. Bit by bit, just start to do even the smallest things in business and life to level up, whether it is taking one class, attaining additional credentials, or networking (which can be done for free). It is amazing how saving just a little every day—packing a lunch, making your own coffee, eating dinners at home, cleaning your own house and clothes, driving an old car—can add up to a lot. You have heard this before. I know that this sounds like trite, old-school wisdom, but it is true all the same. I kept going. I kept believing. I kept saving, saving, saving. In five years, beginning when I started at Juan Juan, I saved $60,000.

I now had the means to set myself up for what I wanted. I chose to invest in my future and attend the Cosmoprof Worldwide industry trade show in Italy. I had espresso-filled conversations with people who, like me, were excited about and devoted to the beauty business. I walked around the booths of vendors, watched makeup artists do magic with color and texture. I found a manufacturer to build my first line of pomades whenever I was ready to greenlight it. The energy and motion was invigorating.

Back at work at Juan Juan, I would walk around Beverly Hills whenever I could spare a minute to look for a space that could accommodate my ideal salon. I was dreaming big now. It would need to be large enough for a proper makeup counter and the people I would hire to work it. I kept walking by an empty space at 438 North Bedford Drive. I learned that the space had been vacant for almost two years, which might work to my advantage, but also that it was managed by a very aggressive landlord. I contacted the broker listed on the advertisement, a younger man who seemed very savvy, to arrange a meeting with this landlord. I filled out the broker's forms about my business and finances, which met his requirements. He set up the meeting with the landlord. When he offered to come with me, I jumped at the opportunity to have someone in my corner.

I quickly found out that no one is a better advocate for you than you are yourself. The broker, Bruce Dembo, and I met at the management office, which was across the street from the vacant space. We were greeted at the door by the landlord, who introduced himself as John. He had that intense, high-energy New York City personality and communication style. He brought us into his office. Bruce and I both sat down in chairs around a small meeting table.

"So, you want to rent the space across the street?" said John. "What do you do?"

"I do eyebrows," I said. He looked directly at me and laughed loudly in my face.

"Whaaat? That's a business? Lady, this is Beverly Hills! Do you think you can pay your rent on eyebrows?"

I waited for Bruce to jump into the conversation and say something about my business, but he just sat there quietly. I could see that he was going to leave it up to me.

"Yes, I will pay my rent and more. Women in Beverly Hills know me. There was an article about me in *Vogue* magazine. My work is already famous. I will make this street famous!" I was mustering all my confidence to talk about my accomplishments. I usually did not talk about myself in this way—I never bragged—but I could see it was not the time for humility. I was becoming desperate to impress him. He laughed at me again.

"Lady, it's a hard no. I've never heard of such a thing!"

I was riled up by this time, insulted at the way he dismissed me. I wanted that space. I *knew* it was the right space for me. The money I had saved was good to qualify for it. I wasn't going to give up. We went back and forth for two hours. All the while,

Bruce sat there and said nothing. No business argument I made seemed to persuade John. Then, I remembered a fundamental truth.

# Business is about relationships, not just balance sheets.

I decided then to just tell him about myself. I told him that I was an immigrant from Romania. I told him about all that had happened for us to get to America, the land of opportunity, and all that had happened since we arrived in LA. The more I talked, the more he became quiet and just listened. He stopped laughing.

"I am sure someone in your family was an immigrant, your parents, your grandparents," I said. "Someone gave them a chance. Give me a chance. Rent me this place for six months," I implored him. "If I don't make it, I will leave. It has been sitting empty for two years, it will probably be empty for six more months or more. Let me have it. Give me a chance. I will prove to you that I will make it."

I could see that my story and passion moved him. I think that he liked that I stood up for myself, that I didn't give up. I am sure that his family had also been immigrants at some point.

"OK, lady. OK. You can have it for six months. I hope I don't regret it!"

I felt elated, triumphant. We began the process of signing the lease at once. Everything I had done led to this moment. I had taken a gamble on myself. I had pushed fate to the edge, turned "no" to "yes." That didn't mean that the way ahead was now clear and easy.

## Turning Points

There are times when we need to forge ahead but there are also times when we need to let go. We all face turning points like these. It is hard to know what to do, but eventually you feel it in your bones. Your internal compass lets you know what the right move is. Victor and I had to acknowledge that we wanted different things, and we needed to permanently part. The year was 1992, and Romania was now opening up to the West. People were finally able to travel back and forth with ease. Victor decided to go home. And my mother decided to join us in LA for an extended period of time and to help with Claudia. Now I could afford to bring her over.

When you live in California, earthquakes are expected to occur. They can be small or seismic, just like all shifts in life. I had just experienced a seismic shift with Victor, but the actual earthquake that hit was so monumental it earned its own name and place in history. The Northridge earthquake was a magnitude 6 7 blind thrust earthquake that occurred on January 17, 1994, at 4:30 a.m., killing fifty-seven people.

I was shaken out of my sleep by a low rumble. I had never felt anything like this before and knew I had to act quickly. I jumped out of bed, woke my mom and Claudia, and grabbed my little go bag, which had my passport, cash, and keys. We managed to get downstairs, to the garage, into the big old Ford, and out to the street before the building came down.

We drove around in our pajamas in a state of shock, Claudia on a blanket, until the following day. We could not get back into the building. Everything was destroyed; we lost all of our possessions. The crystal and porcelain I had brought from Romania was all shattered. The building would later be condemned. We drove through the devastated neighborhood and all the way to Juan Juan, the only place I could think to go. It was just thirteen miles away but not even one bottle was broken. I was reminded that even though immense events or disasters happen every day around the world, tragedies are so local, so personal.

While we were at the salon, a wonderful and generous client reached out and offered us sanctuary at her home in Beverly Hills. We stayed for two weeks figuring out what to do. I found that it was so much easier and more productive living in the heart of my professional world. I had been working seven days a week and commuting more than an hour each way in my old car. With the additional income I could make if I spent that extra hour or so working each day instead of commuting, I calculated that I could afford an apartment in Beverly Hills and a newer used car. The math worked. I found an apartment in Beverly Hills and bought a better car.

The residual effects of the earthquake and the trauma of losing the security of our home base left me frightened and edgy. I thought maybe this was a sign from the universe; maybe I was on the wrong path, maybe I should move back to Romania. With my mother now with me, I realized how much I had missed her, missed my family and my country. Maybe this was the time to go home. The new Romanian government had returned my mother's house and property to her, and she had started to remodel it. We decided that we all would go there for a month to buy furniture and feel it out.

Almost immediately upon arrival in Romania, I realized I didn't fit in the way I once had. I didn't have much in common with my old friends. Being in America had changed me. *Perhaps it is just a fact of life that as we grow, we shed aspects of the people we once were.* I wanted different things now. My work fulfilled me in ways I couldn't even express; it was what I was meant to do. Within a few weeks, Claudia and I were back in LA. Eventually, my mother would sell her house and come to live with us too.

I was soon driving around Beverly Hills in my Mitsubishi Mirage, which was small enough to fit into the tight parking spaces near the salon. It would take over from its predecessor, my beloved old Ford, to transport me around town and onward toward my dreams. When I had flown back into LAX from Romania in the fall of 1994, it felt like I had come home. I had a new sense of confidence and certainty in my choices. The Romanian chapter of my life was truly over. I was looking forward to the rest of the story. Looking forward to Anastasia Beverly Hills.

# Oscar Moment

To *Vogue*, with gratitude,

Our lives are the sum total of many small ordinary moments. There are also the standout events, the super wows, that are so precious they are golden. I call these my Oscar moments. Being profiled by *Vogue* magazine, one of the fashion and beauty world's great influencers, was a showstopper for me. It changed the course of my life.

In 1994, two years after I opened my room at Juan Juan, Marina Rust, a writer for *Vogue*, contacted me for an interview. She had seen an article mentioning me in *Allure*. She wanted to write about me, she said, because "everyone was talking about Anastasia." She came to the salon to meet in person. I offered to do her brows. However, she insisted that she never touched her brows (she did have full beautiful brows). I explained that she couldn't write about my craft unless she experienced the magic herself. I handed her the mirror at the end of the service as I always do. I could see from the dawning smile on her face that she was pleasantly surprised. She loved the results so much that every time she visited LA, she made sure to get her brows done. She was hooked! Her two-page article was so beautifully written it was like a novel.

In the same issue, I recall there was an article on makeup artist Kevyn Aucoin's new book, *Making Faces*, which put a big emphasis on eyebrows. A few pages after this, Marina's story described me as the best-kept secret in Hollywood and talked about how many women were waiting to get their eyebrows done. The pairing seemed almost divinely created. The zeitgeist beckoned both Kevyn and I, and we each stepped into our callings. My brow business took off after that.

This Oscar moment is really two in one. *Vogue* had a deeper meaning for me than Marina Rust could have known at the outset of writing her story. I had come full circle, past and present connecting. After all, when I was a girl in Romania, it had been the smuggled, highly prized, thumb-worn copy of the *Vogue Pattern Book* that helped to elevate my mother's tailoring business. The business that kept us out of poverty. The *Vogue Pattern Book* had been launched with the backing and influence of *Vogue* magazine, lending it a sense of prestige and style. My mother and I designed garments for everyday women based on the glamorous fashions in its pages. Now my name was actually in the magazine. I could never have imagined that the immigrant who arrived in America without any money in her pocket less than a decade earlier would reach this pinnacle. *Vogue* changed my life. Its impact helped put me on the path to becoming who I was meant to be.

# CHAPTER SIX

# Surround Yourself with People You Can Learn From

**Learning never exhausts the mind.**

—Leonardo da Vinci

In May 1997, I went once again to 438 North Bedford Drive to see the space that would become my salon. Walking through the door, I entered a quiet, empty place that seemed poised to fulfill its purpose. It was as if the space itself had decided to remain vacant for two years, turning away all other tenants, just waiting for me to arrive. I stood there alone, silently absorbing its energy. It felt completely right. Natural sunlight lit the interior in a golden hue through its large front windows and glass door. High ceilings soared upward. It had good bones, as we might say in architecture, or in beauty. It had potential. It just needed a loving hand to make it come to life. Using the skills I learned in design school, I set about drawing the blueprints for my ideal layout.

I wanted it to be simple and elegant. I found a contractor who was also a Romanian immigrant to do the remodeling, and a carpenter to build my furniture. I set an opening date for two weeks later, on June 1, 1997. I immediately began telling my customers, rebooking their appointments at the new address, and saying goodbye to the team at Juan Juan. This parting was easier than it had been when I left Giovanna-Jutta as I was an independent business owner cosharing the space, not a staff member, and I was only moving around the block. Juan, John Azar, and all the stylists, it turned out, would continue to be supporters, coming for brow services and referring clients to me.

I decided to call it *Anastasia*, as most other salons seemed to be named for their founders. I spread the word about its opening to the makeup artists and salespeople I knew at the department store cosmetics counters, the stylists at nearby salons, and, of course, all my old colleagues at Giovanna-Jutta. I felt ready for my new beginning, or so I thought.

# There are a million little ways that starting a business is harder than you think it will be.

Starting a business is about the management of details, people, and resources as much as it is a creative endeavor. A founder is like a painter who has the vision of a perfect scene but needs to make a thousand small brush strokes in order to manifest it. Along the way, there are the incredible highs that come from small successes but even more unforeseen challenges, obstacles, and setbacks. Right from the get-go, I had challenges.

I was pleased with the remodeling; the soft colors imbued the space with the mixture of sophistication and calm I wanted to project. The smaller private treatment rooms were well proportioned. The whole look was airy and elevated, illuminated by sunshine. I designed the space to be an invitation to a luxury experience. I wanted every woman to feel beloved, like a goddess, and even more so, to feel like a dear friend. A place where she felt at home.

Two weeks is a fast turnaround for any construction project, but it was going well and was on target for our deadline until the day before my opening. The major remodeling was completed and the salon interior looked lovely. The equipment for the facial rooms, brow station, and hairdressers' chairs had been delivered. But the furniture for the waiting room and the hair stations had not arrived.

I was worried but not yet in a panic. Early in the morning, I phoned the company that was making the furniture. There was no answer. I called all day long, still no answer. They seemingly had disappeared, entirely vanished from the face of the earth. I didn't know then that it would be another month before they answered my call, and a month after that before my furniture finally arrived.

I called again for the final time from my apartment late that night, again no answer. I hung up the wall phone in the kitchen; its long curly cord was twisted into a tight knot from my pacing back and forth. My heart sank. People already knew about the opening, clients were booked. The date couldn't be changed. I had no idea what to do now. I walked out to my living room. My mother was sitting there in one of my newly purchased chairs, holding Claudia. It was such a comfort to see her face at a time like this. I had enjoyed decorating my Beverly Hills apartment, purchasing a few pieces of nicer furniture than I previously had in Sherman Oaks. I wanted so much to entertain guests at home, as I once did in Romania. I looked around the room and thought to myself, *Well, this furniture is . . . presentable.* It could work in a pinch until I could get the furniture that I had commissioned. "Mom, I need to make some more calls," I said. "It is going to be a long night."

## An Entrepreneur Turns Mistakes into Magic

The people I had been able to call in to help arrived early at my apartment. They carried nearly everything I had to the street and loaded it into several vans. We drove together to the salon and carefully brought all the furniture inside. I spread the pieces out strategically so that to a casual eye it would look minimalist and purposeful, not the last-minute, feverish attempt at filling the space that it was. My living room couch with potted plants on either side of it actually made the waiting area look welcoming. When all the pieces were in place, I looked around the sparsely filled room. It was not the perfect presentation I had wanted for my first day, but I knew it was the best I could do under the circumstances. Even so, I felt sad about how it looked. It was one of the most important days of my life with my future riding on the outcome. First impressions can often make or break a business. After having enthusiastically talked about the new salon for more than a month, I hoped that this scene would not disappoint my clients. The many helpers now went off to start their own mornings. I walked into one of the private rooms to calm myself. I breathed deeply for a few precious seconds and whispered a little prayer. It seemed like the right moment to invite in grace. But there was no time to linger.

I opened the door at 9:00 a.m. and my clients began to trickle inside. I greeted each of them, my heart beating so loudly I thought they surely heard it. Miraculously, everyone who entered looked as if they had walked into an enchanted world and commented about how much they loved the "homey" atmosphere. I stood there smiling, like a swan who glides gracefully across the water while frantically pedaling underneath to stay afloat. Much to my relief, I had turned a mistake into magic and pulled this one off. It always seems that those who are successful in their fields—the top gymnast, dancer, soccer player, fashion designer, CEO—make what they do look effortless. Of course, it isn't. Underneath, there's a lot of sweat, willpower, determination, and resilience that goes into any success. Success is full of effort, never effortless.

Now that we were open the real work began, and it never stopped. When it is your business, nine to five becomes 24/7. I worked around the clock to make everyone who walked in the door walk out feeling cared for, cared about, and uplifted. Even when the salon closed at the day's end, I was still thinking about how I could make it better tomorrow. The models and celebrities who had been my clients previously followed me to the new salon, mixing a sprinkle of their stardust into the golden sunshine filling the space. For that, I will always be grateful.

Two weeks after I opened, my landlord, John, called from his office across the street to tell me that he had been observing my salon.

"Lady, I come to my office at eight in the morning; there are people outside waiting for your salon to open. When I leave my office at night, there are still people waiting to get in. What do you do again?"

"I told you I do brows."

"Yeah, OK, OK." There was a long pause and then he said, "This is the most incredible place in Beverly Hills, I've never seen anything like it."

"I told you I would make this street famous!" I allowed myself to savor this triumph for a moment. It was very rewarding to know that the clients believed in me. When you see that the result of your work makes people happy, that they are coming back, that they are waiting in line for you, it validates your craft. Being able to serve so many customers from all walks of life filled me with indescribable joy.

Later that week, we had a grand-opening party. It was planned by my friend Bethenny Frankel, who back then was experimenting with different businesses before becoming founder and CEO of Skinnygirl, among other enterprises. She wanted to plan the party for me. Of course, I said yes. Our friends always helped each other. That's Hollywood then and now. We were building an amazing community of women. The party was filled with fabulous drinks, delicious foods, and gorgeous women. The guest list caused quite a buzz.

I could not stop to celebrate for long. I had a business to run, and I was running a marathon. I felt that I had to work harder and do more just to catch up to those who had the head start of being born in America—those who spoke the language perfectly and understood all the cultural nuances and references. If you are born here, it's a different story. You have a different story. I think that my story, feeling behind before I even started, is a common one among immigrants. I keenly felt the need to overcome what I saw as my disadvantages. They circled in the shadows for me: I was not that young, already thirty-nine. I did not fully comprehend the language, which was of critical importance to my business. I did not have experience with the legal, financial, or banking systems. I spoke with an accent (and still do), which can make it difficult to be understood by native speakers. I did not have deep roots in the community, those invaluable connections that support you and help you to solve personal and business challenges.

I could have been intimidated and just given up, but something inside of me was too stubborn to back down. We can allow our "I am nots" to determine our fate or we can decide to grab fate in our two hands and move forward in spite of them. *Destiny is the accumulation of what you decide to do every day.* You can decide to unleash the greatness inside of you. That is what I did. You simply have to take action. Think deeply about what it is you want to do most and take a step toward it. Whether you are trying to be a chef, record a podcast, or set up your own beauty business, you must decide to keep your attention on yourself, not on what others have. You have to say to yourself, *I decide to stay positive; I decide to push through difficult moments, rather than giving up; I decide that I will build my own community of support if there isn't one; I decide to unleash my greatness.*

If I was able to do this given my circumstance and become a successful leader, think of how much you can accomplish. You are already way ahead of where I was when I started. There were so many things I didn't know the day I opened my salon doors, but I knew that I could not do this alone. We all need guidance, mentorship, and help along the way. I knew I had to surround myself with people I could learn from.

> Embrace what you don't know, especially in the beginning, because what you don't know can become your greatest asset.
> It ensures that you will absolutely be doing things different from everybody else.
>
> —Sara Blakely, founder of Spanx

## Small Is the New Big

I started with a small team of talented people. I hired Tino Stan to be the manager of the salon, and he helped me with everything. He was a longtime friend from Romania, since elementary school, and one of the most loyal people I knew. He was a big part of my journey: We worked together for approximately eighteen years. I brought in Cora, a top facialist whom I had also known from Romania; Cynthia and Nathan, two incredible hairstylists I had met at other salons; and my friend Susan Stan, whom I've known since we were fourteen. They joined me as independent contractors under the umbrella of the Anastasia salon, rather than as employees. This business model worked well for my start-up. These practitioners would pay a nominal rent for their "chair," and I would not have the financial weight of employee salaries and other overhead. There is a long tradition in the beauty business of sharing salon space in this manner, just as I had at Juan Juan. I carefully chose the best experts to be on my launch team, as I wanted Anastasia to have a reputation for excellence right from the start. Each already had a customer base from other places that followed them to the salon, and we referred clients to each other.

I kept the business lean and small for a number of years before expanding. One of the best success strategies for a start-up is to develop your services and products while not overextending yourself financially. I never went to business school, but I had learned valuable lessons about managing cash flow from my mother, Giovanna and Jutta, and others. I learned from other nearby salons, stores, restaurants, and owners that over-invested in staff or inventory. Many businesses that trended immediately became shooting stars before fizzling out just as fast as they started. I wanted to create a business that would sustain and survive for years to come. Staying small gives you the ability to pivot as needed, which is crucial. As an entrepreneur, your initial assumptions or strategies are often incorrect. That's why it is important to be adaptable. I was constantly rethinking my plans and asking others for input and advice.

Being an entrepreneur is not just about having an idea; it's about transforming that idea into a thriving and successful business. The only way to accomplish this long-term vision is to relentlessly move forward and to be dedicated to providing excellent service and/or products. Building a prosperous business requires perseverance. Keeping your eye on your goals as well as the task at hand is the key for progress and success. Of course, there will be times when you question your decisions. As an entrepreneur, you face numerous challenges and distractions. It is essential to maintain your determination and not let anything, even achievement, steal your focus from the big picture.

But to build a thriving company and culture, it is also important to share your natural enthusiasm. I always have had a lot of energy, and I try to stay positive and be uplifting to those around me. Even when I am dealing with difficult things, I stay in the present moment and enjoy it. I allow myself to let go, have a laugh with the team, a hug to celebrate a colleague's professional or personal win, or a walk around the block as a break. Integrity, loyalty, and also *joy* are key elements to success and overlooked in business manuals. Exuberance, passion, and elation are contagious. People gravitate toward them.

When you find joy in your work and in your day, you naturally transmit it to everyone around you. I feel blessed and happy every day. As an entrepreneur, I know that how I react, interact, and emote impacts everyone around me, from clients to employees. It is important to be a conscious leader, to choose your words mindfully and inspire your team. If you want to keep employees and customers happy, you must allow your business to be a happy place. I learned this from my mother long ago. It is a universal truth. Business is about sharing and giving, solving problems and offering support. *In the end, it is about love.* As my mother had taught me, long ago: Love what you do, and you will lift others up to be their best selves

When you start or run a business, or lead a team of people in some way, it is OK to admit that you don't have all the answers. Don't be afraid to ask for help and help others as much as possible in return. My clients were happy to share their expertise and their resources. When I couldn't understand the terms in a contract, a client helped to clarify the language. When I needed a lawyer, another client introduced me to hers. My clients shared their challenges with me as well. I would always ask them, "How can I help?" They knew that I was sincere. I would say, "Ask me any question and I will get you an answer within two weeks." My clients would always come through for me and I always came through for them.

# If you give to others with a generous heart, you will receive it back tenfold.

I continued to expand my circle, swapping services with nearby department stores and private makeup artists, other salons, and local businesses: We would send each other clients. The national articles in *Allure* and *Vogue* had given me a boost and taught me that such publicity could create word of mouth beyond the reach of my neighborhood to new people all around LA. I didn't have a publicist, but through my network of journalists and clients, I positioned myself to get more interviews in the local media.

There was also a young generation of TV journalists and reporters sharing stories about beauty, fashion, and celebrities to new entertainment shows such as *Entertainment Tonight*, *E! News*, *Access Hollywood*, and more. Los Angeles was at the center of this lifestyle TV boom, and it had its own vibrant local media market as well. I was in the right place at the right time, doing the right thing that was telegenic. Shaping brows is a visual art and I loved to demonstrate my technique. I was able to communicate with the audience because I could show what I was doing. I also felt the confidence in myself that came from being a master of my craft. Confidence is the best accessory a woman can wear. I became a go-to expert for these style TV shows.

It was at this time that I met two young journalists just starting out on the LA scene, Maria Menounos and Bobbie Thomas, who both went on to have highly successful media careers. Each was smart, caring, and hardworking, which I admired, as well as beautiful. Beloved as the longtime style editor for NBC's *Today* show, Bobbie is an author and a trusted voice in beauty, fashion, and personal transformation known for her heart, humor, and honesty.

Maria is an author, acclaimed reporter, and presenter on a variety of the major entertainment programs. Beyond her work in entertainment, Menounos has been recognized for her resilience and strength. She is dedicated to helping others with her podcast *Heal Squad x Maria Menounos*. Her journey has resonated with so many because she has openly shared her experiences, promoting awareness and support for health-related causes. Menounos is also an entrepreneur, cofounding the digital network AfterBuzz TV, and engages in various philanthropic efforts. Her positive attitude and determination to overcome challenges make her a role model for those facing similar struggles. She has inspired so many people, including me.

Back then, we were all still at the beginning. These two remarkable women were a part of the group of talented stylists, makeup artists, moviemakers, and journalists in whose orbit I found myself. Everyone was trying to connect with other people.

I realized how much I loved connecting women to each other. I believe that everyone has something to teach others and something to learn. I love when wisdom is shared and friendships are formed. I started to wonder if there was a way that I could bring together all these incredible people I was meeting—those who I could learn from as well as those I could possibly help. It was my own dream community.

The concept of "networking" had been a part of the corporate conversation since the 1980s. But it seemed so cold and formal to me. I imagined it as people wearing stuffy suits exchanging hearty handshakes and business cards. I still had the longing to entertain. One day it just clicked that I could combine networking and entertaining. I had come from a culture where this is how you did business. You share a meal, a glass of wine or champagne, and you talk to each other. I decided to host small parties at my home for women I invited to do business together, to collaborate, and to help each other by sharing our experiences, our energies, and our lives. I chose my friends and each of the people I did business with because of their integrity, generous spirit, talent, and joy. I started with a handful of small gatherings of four to five people, but would expand to larger parties too. The circle began here, at this time, with these talented people yearning to make our mark. I was learning, thriving, and finally using my best dishes and glassware. It became a passion and lifelong commitment of mine to mentor other women, in time reaching out to organizations working with young women and starting foundations of my own. Hosting these parties, bringing together people from a variety of industries and interests, is still a major part of my world to this day.

## Position Yourself to Invite In the Extraordinary

Every day is a new day to make something happen, meet someone new, find a new client. We find inspiration in many places. In his role as teacher John Keating in the movie *Dead Poets Society*, Robin Williams said, "Carpe diem. Seize the day, boys. Make your lives extraordinary." The line stayed with me. If I were to make my life and my business extraordinary, I knew that I needed people around me I could rely on to achieve this.

After a few years of steady business growth, I felt ready to hire my own team. There are hundreds of books about how to hire people, MBA courses, special human resources departments dedicated to it. I find that hiring is an alchemical process of melding together information, intuition, and imagination. For me it comes down to these basic factors: talent, passion, and trust. I look for talented people willing to do everything it takes to do the job and beyond, and to be able to trust them to do just that. I have hired family as employees and employees who have become family to me. Loyalty, like joy, is another key element in building your business. A loyal team is critical to success. I believe in building a team of stars and giving them everything they need to shine. My work ethic allows me to lead by example. I expect the same excellence from everyone on my team as I demand from myself.

Over time my core team came together. I hired two experienced general makeup artists and trained them to become brow specialists. Elena Grigore came from the makeup counter at the department store Robinsons-May, and Jasmine Kim did training at MAC Cosmetics and Estée Lauder. Twenty years later, Jasmine is still a top brow specialist with me, and seventeen years

124

later, Elena is manager of the Anastasia Beverly Hills salon. Many of my team, like Alex Goodman, Anita Iknadossian, Tracy Taylor, and Michelle O'Neill, have also been a part of the success of the salon for a number of years.

Many more people would come to play a role in growing the business into Anastasia Beverly Hills, including my daughter. I was now well established and surrounded by an ever-growing circle of support. I was excited to see what would come next.

# The Entrepreneur's Toolkit

I believe being an entrepreneur requires immense dedication and hard work. It is not just about having an idea; it's about transforming that idea into a thriving and successful business. To achieve this, review the following crucial qualities to give yourself an edge.

### Work Is Serious Business, but Don't Take Yourself Too Seriously
If you want to lead others, lighten up, laugh, and let your inner glow show. People are more productive in, and customers are more attracted to, a happy work environment.

### Determination and Persistence Make the Difference Between Lagging and Leadership
It is essential to have both when pushing through unexpected challenges that inevitably arise. Being flexible allows you to adapt and adjust your plans to accommodate and overcome unforeseen circumstances. Every day is a new opportunity to keep moving toward your goals, no matter the obstacle or setback.

### Build Your Circle of Support
Successful entrepreneurs nurture strong relationships. The more people you know, the more you can grow.

### Imagine Greatness in Others
Nurture the talents of the people who work with you. Use your imagination to see their potential and help them find roles in your company that unleash their greatness.

# PART TWO

# If there is no seat at the table, make your own table.

The beauty industry could not imagine there was a
billion-dollar market waiting to be built. They did not
know there was a need until I showed them what could
be done. Don't let anyone with bad eyebrows tell you
how to live your life. If you believe it, find your own way
to make it happen.

CHAPTER SEVEN

# Your Customer Is Your Boss

**People will forget what you said, people will forget what you did, but people will never forget how you made them feel.**

—MAYA ANGELOU

There is an exchange of energy that happens when you make somebody feel beautiful. I know this from experience with my clients. I believe in this sacred contract with my whole being: heart, mind, and soul. No matter how hard I worked or the business challenges I faced, when I handed the client the mirror at the end of my service and saw a smile as bright as a sunrise dawn across their face, I felt their joy. Every single time. It motivated me to do more. I spent every waking hour thinking about what my clients needed and wanted.

I learned an immutable business truth from my mother's shop that is applicable whether you are an entrepreneur, vendor, receptionist, middle manager, corporate mogul, or anything else: The customers make your business succeed. It's not about *you*; it's about *them*. I may be the CEO, but I work for Anastasia Beverly Hills. I came from a culture where this is how business is done and always will be. My relationships with my clients are based on trust and integrity. Nothing is more important than integrity in business and in life. My clients knew without a doubt that they could always count on me to do everything I could and more to help them look and feel beautiful. Their loyalty gave me confidence that I was on the right path.

# Great brows don't happen by chance, they happen by appointment.

It had been more than a year since I first opened my salon. My clients would come every three weeks to refresh their brows, booking their ongoing appointments in advance. Connecting with each other this frequently allowed us to shape enduring friendships as well as brows. It gave me the opportunity to perfect not only their experience but their customized brow shape itself. I had many celebrity clients at this point, just to name a few: Kirstie Alley, Jennifer Aniston, Kate Capshaw, Naomi Campbell, Penélope Cruz, Laura Dern, Lauren Holly, Helen Hunt, Heidi Klum, Jennifer Lopez, Madonna, Elle Macpherson, Julianna Margulies, Claudia Schiffer, Sharon Stone, Rita Wilson, and Reese Witherspoon. Each one was a spectacular beauty with an iconic signature look.

I wanted to sculpt the ideal brow for each one and provide results they could depend on. I was obsessed with this challenge and determined to figure it out. Instantly seeing in my mind's eye the shape of the perfect brow that would enhance someone's beauty was my unusual ability, my gift. People sometimes thought that I was looking at them so deeply because I saw something wrong. That could not be further from the truth. I never judge someone. What I am actually doing when looking at someone is thinking about what shape will complement their face—what the golden ratio of their face is. It is like in the movie *The Sixth Sense*, only I could see *brows*, not dead people. The famous painter and sculptor Michelangelo once explained the process of creating his masterpiece, the statue of the biblical figure of David. He said, "I created a vision of David in my mind and simply carved away everything that was not David." I could do the same with brows. I had a vision of a particular brow in my mind, and I could carve away everything that was not that shape.

Eyebrows are the framework for the entire face. The busier I became in working with clients and in training others in the salon, the more I began to wonder if there was a way to template my golden ratio eyebrow shaping technique to make it easier for makeup artists and other team members to follow my method and for my clients to re-create their perfect brow at home in between appointments.

I remembered a Romanian artist, an old man, whom I admired as a young woman. I loved to watch him work. I don't remember his name, but the impression he made on me was indelible. My mother would hire him every two years to paint the walls of our house; that's how I met him. He would restore old churches and formal buildings, using stencils to mimic magnificent Corinthian columns and other intricate features using all sorts of amazing colors. A stencil is an outline of an image, with a cut-out shape inside that can be filled in. An artist applies paint or ink over it, pulls the stencil away, and a precise shape or pattern is left behind.

This artist once even gave me some of his pastel blue-green pigments, as well as pearlescent pigment, and black charcoal to make my own eye shadow and eyeliner. That delighted my teenage soul, as we had no access to formal makeup.

I began to draw a few common brow shapes, using the golden ratio principles, on transparent sheets of paper as templates. I named these my *stencils*, inspired by that old Romanian artist. Instead of using paints for my brow art, I would fill the open space within the outline with pencil, powder, or pomade, applying it in small hairlike strokes. I would tweeze stray hairs to enhance the natural brow shape, carefully wax or trim around the edges for a more precise line, and brush the brow hair up to dramatically lift the features. Clients loved the effect, and I loved that I could consistently create the look they wanted.

I was still using my homemade pomade of Vaseline, aloe vera, and eye shadow. I would often hear, "My eyebrows look perfect when I leave, but after I take a shower, the pomade washes away. I need something to apply at home between appointments." More and more clients asked me for products. I was getting ready to take that step, saving every penny I could to be able to move ahead when the time was right.

## The Road Ahead Is Dark Until Fate Sends You a Light

The light that pushed me forward was a sparkly, delightful young actress named Poppy Montgomery. Poppy had come to LA from Australia and was a breath of fresh air. I loved everything about her style, her thick red hair, her natural beauty, her effervescent personality. She would be very successful, I thought. I had been working with her for a while when she told me that she was going to go to Canada to film a made-for-television movie in 2001 titled *Blonde*, where she would portray actress Marilyn Monroe. She—and her agent—wanted me to style her brows. However, she would need to keep her brows exactly the same for at least six months while she was filming. The film's makeup artist needed to work with her to replicate what I had created as, of course, it was impossible for me to be there on set. It was a watershed moment for me. For the first time, I had to explain my techniques to someone outside of my salon.

It touched me deeply that Poppy put her trust in me to help her for this role that would be so important to her career. There was no way that I would let her down. Fortunately, Poppy had shared this with me well in advance of her departure date. I used every second to think about this challenge. I went to the art store and bought some thin, flexible plastic. I cut it into the shapes that I used for Poppy's brows. These became my first plastic stencils. I put them into a small bag with a pot of my pomade in her color, an angled brush, tweezers, and a small pair of scissors. I gave this to her along with specific instructions detailing how the makeup artist could re-create Poppy's perfect golden ratio brow. Six months later, Poppy returned from the set and sat in my chair. It had worked!

"Oh my God, Anastasia. This was amazing!" she said about the tools I had given her. "You should make a kit like this because there are so many women who can't come to Beverly Hills. And this was so helpful!"

She bubbled with enthusiasm like the frothiest champagne; I just wanted to hug her. It was the jolt I needed. I realized that my business had reached a pivot point. I could remain the owner of a very successful salon, or I could expand to new horizons. I knew that I wanted more. Reaching women around the country and even around the world was what I wanted. I summoned the courage and the will to continue the journey. I was filled with hope, a sense of promise, and a degree of naivety. Success is a journey, not a destination. I knew I had to keep moving forward and learning. I had no idea how much learning was truly ahead for me.

## There Is More to Bringing Products to Market Than Having a Dream, an Idea, or a Passion

If you want to create a product, a service, or add something new to the business or organization you are in, where would you begin?

Close your eyes for a minute and imagine:

*Who is your customer?*
*What do they want? Who do they aspire to be?*
*What needs are going unmet in the marketplace?*
*What would your product or service be?*
*How would you deliver it: in a store, at a fair, a spa, online?*
*What would your brand stand for?*

Breathe. Write your answers down. Repeat.

These are the questions I asked myself, dreamed about, meditated on. I didn't rush; I took time to become truly grounded. I remembered who I was and what I believed in; where I had come from and where I still wanted to go. For the products I wanted to create, I began to imagine how they would serve my customer, how they would reflect my standards and values. I put myself into what I would describe as a "service mindset," which is a customer-first point of view. What were their needs and desires? Even more importantly, how could I help them feel and look their best? For me, my innovations had always come from trying to solve a problem for my customer. Even for the customers I didn't have just yet.

# Brows are the one thing you can do to get into shape without working out.

I had been accustomed to working with my clients one-on-one. To scale up, I would have to teach my techniques in a way that someone who was not sitting in my chair could follow. This was a huge shift. I thought about how my celebrity clients inspired me and validated my work by supporting me for so many years. They inspired other women who saw them in magazines or on the screen. They had the perfect golden ratio faces, the most beautiful eyebrow arches, and amazing bone structure. I had found my hand-drawn stencils inspired by their brow shapes to be such a useful addition to my brow craft. I began to think about how every woman in the world would be able to enhance her own beauty if only she had the right tools. I wanted to mold my client's brow shapes into stencils anyone could use as a map or guide.

How could I create something that could be universally used? How would I get it to someone far away and teach her how to use it? You need to shape eyebrows according to your own bone structure and natural eyebrow shape. I felt my passion growing to share with all women something I truly believed: Brows are a lifestyle, not just a trend. I looked at all the stencils I had drawn thus far. I realized that there was a common starting point: the arch. As a reminder, brows should begin directly above the middle of your nostrils; they should end where the corner of the nostril connects with the outer corner of the eye; and the highest point of the arch should connect with the middle of the iris. Using the golden ratio I developed for eyebrows and calculating for the standard deviation based on the individual's personal bone structure, I narrowed all my sketches and all the possible eyebrow shapes down to five stencils that customers could use as guides for their brow shape. I named each of these stencils: Petite Arch, Slim High Arch, Middle Arch, High Arch, and Full Arch.

I decided on the products that would be in the Anastasia Beverly Hills launch lineup:

**Stencils:** I wanted them to be made in a flexible plastic with three markings aligning with the three points of the golden ratio method to take the guesswork out of achieving a balanced eyebrow shape. Balance and proportion are the foundation of the Anastasia Beverly Hills Golden Ratio Method. The shape of the eyebrow is tailored to your unique features. With a few simple steps, your brows will outlast any trend.

**Powder, Pomade, and Pencils:** I produced these in the most universal shades: taupe, soft brown, medium brown, dark brown, and ebony.

**Specialty Brush:** The last product was a brush that had been forming in my mind for a long time. I had been buying brushes from the art store and experimenting with the best way to use them for brows. I had found that by cutting the bristles into an angle, I could apply my pomade or even eye shadow in small consistent strokes that looked natural and hairlike, creating the perfect results. By this time, with my application techniques honed to ten minutes, I saw between sixty and eighty clients per day. I needed to be quick and precise in order to accommodate my bookings. I designed my caddy, the rolling tray on which I placed wax and other tools, in such a way as to not waste movements. I would use the brush with the angled bristles to fill in the eyebrows, put it down, and then pick up the generic mascara spoolie to complete the look. I found this to be cumbersome, particularly when it was so important to be efficient with all my moves. The idea came to me that the best solution would be to combine these two into one tool: a two-sided brush with the angled bristles on one side and the spoolie on the other. Later, I would use a similar double-sided form to create my Perfect Brow Pencil—working with the manufacturer to create the first duo pencil in the beauty industry—with a pencil on one side and spoolie on the other.

## My number 7B brush would be the first double-sided eyebrow brush ever invented.

I want to take a moment to reflect on my journey with the 7B brush, which I proudly consider the first double-sided eyebrow brush ever invented. It was in the late 1990s. This tool was an innovation in the beauty industry that inspired many imitations and replicas. Its convenience has made it a popular choice among makeup artists and enthusiasts alike.

Looking back, one of the biggest mistakes I made was not trademarking or patenting this groundbreaking invention. At that time, my focus was on problem-solving in the salon, working closely with my clients, and saving diligently for the future. I was hesitant to spend a lot of money on legal fees and opted for an inexpensive attorney to draft a contract between me and a distributor. Little did I know that lawyers often specialize in different areas—corporate law, employment law, and, crucially, trademark and patent law.

I should have sought out a competent trademark attorney and patent attorney to protect my intellectual property. The consequence? Other companies were able to replicate my two-sided brush concept, leading to almost every major beauty brand now featuring their own version of my invention. This experience taught me a very costly lesson: the importance of hiring the right specialists.

Investing in the right legal support is crucial for any entrepreneur. Even if it feels challenging to afford, it's essential to prioritize spending on professionals who can help you not only build your business but also protect it. This is not an area where you should cut corners. Properly setting up your patents and trademarks is vital.

In an era where information is readily available at our fingertips, take advantage of the internet to do your research. The upfront investment in the right specialists will save you significant headaches—and expenses—down the line. I learned this lesson the hard way, but later on, I made it a priority to find and hire the top experts who truly had my best interests at heart.

Let my experience serve as a reminder: Protect your innovations and invest wisely in your business's foundation. Your hard work deserves the right safeguards!

> 66
>
> **I forgot how much work it actually is to start a company. It's A LOT of work.... You've got to come up with a logo. In addition to designing the product: You've got to figure out what to design. You've got to figure out how you're going to get it to the marketplace.... You've got to set up charts, general ledgers, get a management information system ... all this stuff.**
>
> —Steve Jobs
>
> 99

## Business Moves Forward by Grind and Grit

Now that I had my product ideas, it was time to reconnect with the contacts I met at Cosmoprof Worldwide. I went to Italy again, to Bologna. Once again over espressos, we talked about my potential products. Right then, I hit a huge challenge to my plans. There were different manufacturers for the different products, but they had one thing in common: All of them wanted cash up front and had a stipulated advance order quantity for a start-up. This can be a major hurdle for an unknown brand or new business, particularly if you want to manufacture abroad where you don't have deep relationships. A new business has to prove its viability to vendors, factories, and sometimes even warehouse facilities before they will take you on as a client and do work for you on credit. The only way to play is to pay.

I have my own beliefs about money. When to save it, when to use it. Money funds dreams, not things. But they need to be the right dreams. I went back home to gather my thoughts and to decide for certain if I was really 100 percent–plus committed to doing this. There is always uncertainty in starting a new venture, whether you're making a bet on your future for the first time or abandoning a road you started down for another path. I'm all for taking big leaps, but I think it's absolutely necessary to evaluate those risks from every angle, so you can take and make them with calculated confidence.

You have to probe things from all sides: How much money can I afford to allocate to a new venture while still being able to hold a comfortable amount of cash in reserve? Will I still have enough resources to keep my company going through the start-up phase? What will it also cost in time, energy, and personnel? If you can make the investment in a new venture while still having a cash safety net and resources to keep your core business going, you have mitigated the risk to some degree. If you must go all in, you might want to pause and rethink. Do this math for yourself, if you are starting or expanding your business. I guarantee you will not be sorry that you investigated from all angles. Another way to put it is to only bet as much as you can afford to lose.

The final part of the calculation is do you *want to*? Do you believe it is the right next move for you? I decided, in this case, to move forward. I bought, renovated, and sold houses in LA to add additional cash into the business. This would become my pattern: investing, reinvesting, scrimping, saving. I was blessed that real estate in LA would always increase in value and I seemed to have a knack for choosing locations.

I went back to Italy and contracted with all the manufacturers for my initial product runs. It took time to find the right plastic for the stencils, the right pomade and pencil formula that would stay consistent, and the right width and length of the brush. Fortunately, I had my own built-in opportunity for market research and focus groups. The manufacturers would send samples to me for my approval (still to this day, I approve every single batch of makeup for quality control). I would bring everything to the salon to test, making sure the colors and formulas were just right, the five stencils were as universal and easy-to-use as I wanted, and the brush was perfection in my hands. My clients and my salon team loved being a part of the process, and their feedback was invaluable to help me create my signature products.

## Rules Rule the Industry

When you are starting a company, organization, or endeavor, you have to learn as much as you can about every aspect of it. Do your homework. The more aware you are of the hot issues and problems in the industry you're operating in, the easier it will be for you to make the best decisions and save time and money in the long run. Every industry has its own idiosyncrasies, ways of behaving, unique features, and attributes that must be learned in order to do business. Just as each country has its own customs that need to be observed for harmonious relationships.

I had never studied business in a formal way; I had relied on my instincts to carry me. Now, I was in the deep end of the pool without a lifeguard. I found the rules and requirements for the cosmetics industry to be particularly intricate. This is due to the fact that our products are applied on a person's eyes, hair, or skin. There are many domestic and international regulations that must be followed. The formulas and packaging need to be created in just such a way that products remain stable. There are shipping duties, tariffs, and restrictions when bringing products to the US from overseas. I hired a 3PL company, or a third-party logistics provider, which is a service that businesses use to handle logistics and supply chain management such as the receiving of inventory, storage, fulfillment of orders, and invoicing. All this, of course, required the use of attorneys, accountants, and the founding of new departments like procurement and sales.

And this was just the beginning.

I maintained calm on the outside, but there were days when inside I felt a sense of overwhelm. Other days excitement pulsed through me, bright and electric. The business and I were growing in new and uncharted ways; sometimes in starts and stops as I had to figure out the right next step. I had a lot of advisers and employees around me now, but I still wanted to follow my intuition. In business, you need to listen to your intuition. If something doesn't feel right, it probably isn't. I believe that all leaders, thinkers, managers, and entrepreneurs must listen to their gut if they realize something isn't right. At the end of the day, it is your responsibility to keep the company or organization solvent, and your staff motivated, happy, and employed.

In tough or challenging times, I would take a few moments to course correct: to breathe and be grateful for the fact that I had such abundance around me. I would listen to that inner voice that said, *You are OK. You are enough.*

Jim Rohn, the motivational speaker, said, "You are the average of the five people you spend the most time with." I chose my friends, colleagues, and business partners because they also believed in the same standard of integrity, trust, loyalty, and hard work as me. I knew they would help me grow the business, and we could grow together. I believe that a business or organization has its own life force that must be constantly fed, maintained, and nurtured. This life force, this energy, is the engine that generates business success. If after a couple of years you are not busy or acquiring new customers at a steady rate, stop and analyze why not. It is crucial to figure out which gear in the machine is not functioning at maximum capacity: staff, location, investment, learning and development, or the product. Is your team distracted or complacent? If your business is not moving forward, it is dying. You need to adjust. Pivot. Add fuel where needed. As a leader, you create the momentum and the atmosphere.

At the end of the day, your clients and your employees are the two important parts of your business. Both need your care for your business to thrive. Give them your energy, your positivity, and your love. Reinvest the money you make in creating exceptional products for your customers and in hiring exceptional people who take care of your business the way you take care of them.

Talent is important, but those intangible traits of integrity, trust, loyalty, and hard work are also keys to driving business success.

*Do your employees or team share your vision?*

*Will they offer their ingenuity in ways that go beyond their job description?*

*Will they help to foster a collaborative and creative work environment?*

*Do they value your customer the same way that you do?*

Everyone who interacts with your customer—whether your manager or those who respond to emails—makes a difference in how they experience your products, service, or brand. Your customer is your boss. Rule #1: *Always Protect Your Client.*

## Becoming Anastasia Beverly Hills

I knew without a doubt that that my products would be beautifully packaged. They would be star quality, Hollywood worthy. I wanted them to be inspirational and aspirational, and to feel as if a woman had the luxurious elegance of my salon on her vanity table or in her purse. Upscale. Sophisticated. Gorgeous. I hired a design team, headed by Etienne, who were inspired by the challenge. I drew the logo I saw in my mind's eye: an italic A with a butterfly on top. Etienne and I spent days together in his garden with color palettes and type, experimenting to find the perfect packaging. I love flowers; the many varieties are each uniquely beautiful, like my customers. Inspired by the blooms in his garden, we finally came up with the logo and packaging design. I was thrilled. Until it landed on the desk of my new attorney, Daniel Cislo of Cislo & Thomas LLP.

Daniel was a lovely man, very straightforward. We sat together in his glass-windowed office, overlooking the city.

"We have a problem," he said to me. My heart sank. I was pretty far into the process at this point.

"We can't trademark a name. *Anastasia* is not unique, there are millions of Anastasias. You need to have a good trademark, one that can be enforced and protected around the globe. We need to have something else besides your name to differentiate your company."

I found this confusing. Maybe I just didn't understand. "My salon is Anastasia," I reminded him.

"Yes, that's for a business in LA. Now with products, you will need to be able to build a presence everywhere around the world. If you want to call your company just *Anastasia* in South America or southern Europe or any place else, we will be constantly hiring lawyers in each country to protect it. With the right trademark we won't have to do that. We need it to be a combination of words that no one else has or can have."

"What do you mean?"

"What if you added a location to it? What if you added the words *Beverly Hills*?"

"Anastasia Beverly Hills." I repeated it to myself several times.

Of course, this is the moment in the movie where we expect fireworks to occur, when trumpets blare, when we feel chills and the predestiny of future success. However, that wasn't the case. I wasn't sure I liked it. I had to sit with it for a while and say it out loud more than once: Anastasia Beverly Hills. There was a certain cadence to the words. There was a strong connection to my salon and my life. After all, when I came to America, I specifically came to LA. When I chose a location for the salon, I was determined that it would be in Beverly Hills. Beverly Hills certainly had world-famous recognition as well as a personal meaning for me.

"But what will it mean to the customer?" I said, after a time. My mind, as always, returning to the needs of the customer: *It was not about me, it was about them.* The Anastasia salon was well-known for brows in LA. But what would the name Anastasia Beverly Hills mean to women across the country and around the world? It was the most important question to me.

"You need to make Anastasia Beverly Hills synonymous with eyebrows," he said, rather simply. "And then it will mean *everything.*"

We looked at each other and I nodded my approval. My company was now Anastasia Beverly Hills. A new vision hovered around me and came into view. He was correct, of course, and I am thankful for his input. I opened the salon in 1997. Twenty plus years later, the company is synonymous with eyebrows and many more beauty innovations. But in the late 1990s, the way to achieve that was still unclear to me. I was determined to build Anastasia Beverly Hills into *the* brow brand. It would take every ounce of time, energy, resources and some stardust to make it happen.

# Oscar Moment

## My First Products

There is something special about a first experience. I would go on to present hundreds of products, used by millions of people, with distribution in countless countries around the world. And each one is important to me. However, these first products in the Anastasia Beverly Hills line laid the foundation for everything to come. They were a result of my focus on early clients, who tested and proved them, as well as the efforts of talented artists who worked with me. Each product's existence, its inception and launch, was an Oscar moment in my life. They were at once the fulfillment and the beginning of a dream.

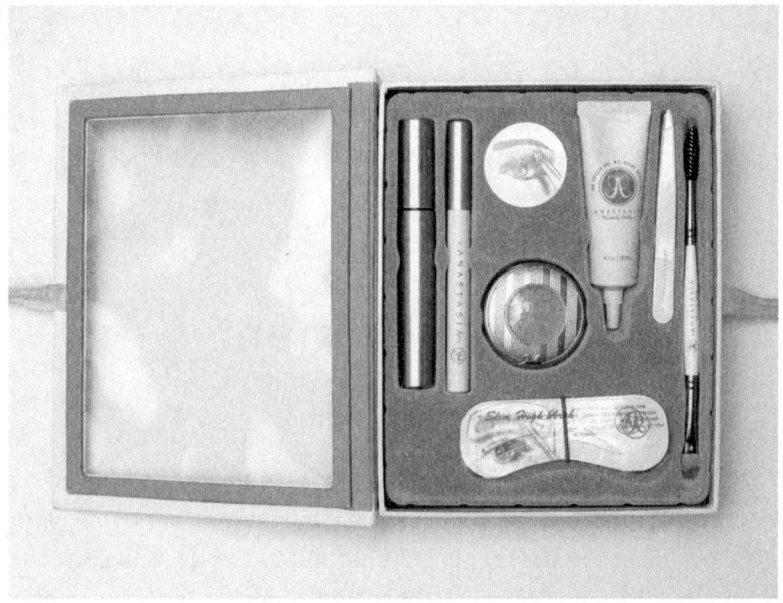

**First brow kit, 1999, included clear brow gel, highlighter pencil, brow powder, stencils, tweezers, dual-ended brush, and after-tweeze cream.**

**From left to right: blush, pressed powder, loose powder compacts**

# CHAPTER EIGHT

# Be Ready for Your Moment

**Miracles come in moments. Be ready and willing.**

—WAYNE DYER

It was mid-morning in March 1999. The salon was already buzzing with women talking and phones ringing. I loved that sound. It lifted me up and kept me going. I looked out at all the activity from my own station at the back of the large open room that was decorated in golds and pinks. Simple. Elegant. A space clients could open themselves into, feel safe to share their stories and, of course, to get their eyebrows groomed. My clients often told me that the conversation was one of the reasons they kept coming back.

There were two other stations, or chairs as we called them, where my hand-picked and trained estheticians were working with clients. The salon had three private rooms for waxing treatments. The round department-style counter in the center of the room was bustling with clients receiving final makeup touches before walking out onto North Bedford Drive. Beyond the counter was the reception area with one small bench and two chairs that were always occupied. There was already a line of walk-ins and women waiting for their appointments. Golden light streamed through the glass door—the legendary California sunshine, which had reached across continents, beckoning me to America and illuminating my dreams. It's been said that it's always sunny in Southern California. It was true.

Waiting for the right moment between clients, I went to the private room at the back of the salon. The space, filled from bottom to top with supplies, was also a small office. On the desk were phone messages for me. One immediately stood out: It said that *The Oprah Winfrey Show* had called! There was a phone number below. I barely moved. My entire body tingled. *The Oprah Winfrey Show* was, of course, the most influential show on television. More than that, Oprah was a hero to me. After all, when I first moved to America, her show had kept me company as a young mother at home. Oprah's own background, overcoming many challenges, was an inspiration to me. If she could find her way, so could I. In my early days in America, I would often ask myself, "What would Oprah do?"

I looked in the small mirror we kept in the room for our own touch-ups. My makeup and brows reflected the techniques I had perfected. I wore a tailored black dress, pearls, and four-inch-high heels. I always dressed fashionably, with my hair and makeup styled, to show respect to my clients. It was now part of the salon experience they came to expect from us. I took a deep breath. I sat down at the desk and picked up the phone.

I spoke with one of the show's producers. The conversation was quick. Oprah wanted me to shape her eyebrows *live* in front of the studio audience and the rest of the world who tuned in to her show. This was the moment when fate truly called to me. This was everything I had been working toward. I could hardly believe it: *Oprah knew who I was!* I immediately said, "Yes, of course!" She also asked if we had enough product inventory to handle the volume of requests generated by viewers. They were already used to their shows causing a sensation of sales that made books, movies, and other goods bestsellers.

I thought about Oprah's face and her beautiful, full eyebrows. I had done beauty demonstrations on TV before and had already been interviewed many times by now. But this was different, of course. This was one of the most watched shows on TV. Oprah was an icon, and I was one of her biggest fans. I had already said yes and could not back out. I was being pushed forward toward something unknown. Was I truly ready for this?

## When in Doubt, Arch It Out

Still, I wondered: *How will I handle being on a live TV show on such a big scale?* I thought about it all day as I worked and all that night. In the quiet of my bedroom, I thought about my past, the shadows from my life in Romania that still lingered. I thought about how far I had come from where I started and how long it had taken. I was not an overnight success; there is no such thing. There is a mistaken belief that successful people are just lucky, and that success is something that happens to you: no effort, no great sacrifice, no years of labor involved. That people in any industry or artistic pursuit can just easily become an icon like Jennifer Lopez, a visionary entrepreneur like Steve Jobs or Jeff Bezos, or a legendary sports figure like David Beckham, Nadia Comăneci Conner, or Serena Williams. Nothing is further from the truth. Success takes focus, intention, and drive. As my grandfather once said to me, "Sia, the harder you work, the 'luckier' you get." Like everyone else, I worked for years to get to this big moment. Now, at breakfast, I shared my news with my mother and Claudia.

After we hugged each other with the sheer excitement of it all, Claudia said, "Mom, do you understand what this means?"

"No, what does it mean?"

"Oprah has said repeatedly on her show that she doesn't like to get her eyebrows waxed because it's painful. She's had bad experiences before. What if she doesn't like it and everyone sees that live?" Claudia continued. "What are you going to do?"

"I don't know," I said. I really didn't. We all sat together eating in silence.

Then, it became clear to me. I couldn't let fear stop me: fear of embarrassment, fear of failure. Fear that I could lose everything. I had done everything in my power to get to this moment. I knew my purpose. My art. My craft. I knew what I would have to do. I would summon every ounce of my gumption, my gusto, and embrace this opportunity. To trust that my skills would carry me through, and that Oprah would like the results of my work, I had to believe in myself.

## Oscar Moment: *The Oprah Winfrey Show*

Most of our memories seem to blur over time; the big emotions and hard edges become softer. It is the human condition. A way for us to heal, to grow, to move forward. But then there are the singular times in our lives that stand out forever crystal clear, bold, bright, and sharp. Memories that remain so vivid, they feel like we could almost touch them. Appearing on *The Oprah Winfrey Show* for the first time was one of these moments. An Oscar moment, and one that changed my life.

Soon after my conversation with the producer, I flew from LAX to Chicago, which was the home of Oprah's operations and where the show was televised. I could hardly eat, drink, or talk on the flight. I looked out the window through the clouds at the cities and terrain passing below and kept saying to myself: "You can do this, you can do this, you can do this, you can do this." I took a taxi from O'Hare International Airport to Harpo Studios, which took up an entire city block. I was greeted by the producer in the lobby and immediately ushered backstage to the green room, which is the waiting area for guests who would appear on the show. It was a small comfortable room with an overstuffed couch, a side table with an assortment of beverages, trays of fruit and pastries, and a private bathroom. I handed my tools and kit to the producer, who whisked them away.

I learned then that my segment of the show would be filmed in Oprah's makeup room. When it was time, the producer led me from the green room and down the hallway. Despite our friendly conversation, my body was trembling and I felt like I would faint. We soon stopped in front of an open door and went inside. There she was! Oprah stood up to greet me with a welcoming hug. She couldn't have been nicer. I was so familiar with her face from TV and magazines, but now in person, I stared for a moment, truly taking her in. I imagined what I would create on such a beautiful canvas. What brow shape would most enhance her features. The producers had assembled my tools on a caddy by the side of her makeup chair, even warming the wax to the right temperature, as if we were in the salon.

I was overwhelmed at meeting my idol, and I felt a little intimidated. I was very aware of the fact that I had started to sweat. But the moment I dipped the stick in the wax, my professionalism and skill just took over. I believe that when you are confident in your skills and show that strength to your client, anyone who sits in your chair will feel at ease. I became centered and calm and began to do what I did every day. Today Oprah was my client. I focused on her, the way I would with any client. I said, "Oprah, I want you to close your eyes and relax. There will be no pain. I promise."

The moment she felt my confidence and strength, I could see her soften and sit back. It's the hardest thing to do eyebrows; as a pair, they need to be symmetrical—not mirror images per se, but sisters. To create this symmetry, you have to look directly at somebody's face and turn their face as you work. Unlike being at the salon, I now had to do my work from an unusual angle. In order to show the TV audience what I was doing, I had to stand to one side so I didn't block the camera. What made it possible for me to do this was my many years of experience. When you do something over and over for so long, as I had done with brows, it becomes completely natural to you. You take on what athletes, dancers, and musicians call muscle memory. It is like when you first drive on the freeway, you look around for landmarks and at your GPS to remember your exit. But after driving the same route for many years, you don't even think about it. You just know when to slow down, you know when to exit. I think that was the sense that came over me; I didn't need to follow a GPS, I *knew*. I felt like I went into a state of hypnosis. I've done so many brows, I could almost do them with my eyes closed. I switched into that mode. I did Oprah's right eyebrow and then I moved to the left brow.

"Is it OK?" I asked her.

"Come on, are you plucking?" she said.

"Yes, definitely."

"There is no pain!"

When I was done with the service, I gave her the mirror as I usually do for my clients to show her the results. I watched as she smiled in surprise and delight. That megawatt Oprah smile. The smile that changed my life.

Later, I was invited to sit in the studio audience as they aired the taped segment live for the world to see. Oprah introduced it. "I hate getting my eyebrows plucked," she announced in her marvelous, deep voice, "but before the show Anastasia got her hands on my brows. Normally—it's like pulling teeth, pulling my brows . . . so I just walk around with furry brows. But I never knew the difference before today. This is what they looked like before." They showed a picture of Oprah on the screen. "And this is what they looked like afterwards. What an eyebrow! Unbelievable!"

"Thank you so very much!" she called out to me from the stage.

"You're very welcome!" I replied. I couldn't believe that Oprah was speaking to me in front of everyone! "I'll have to come to LA now . . . to get myself plucked!" she said back to me.

"Anytime!" I answered, truly hoping that she would one day come to the salon.

A month later, Kate Capshaw and Ellen DeGeneres appeared on her show promoting their movie *The Love Letter*. Oprah looked at Kate and said "I know those eyebrows! She did them. I can tell they are her brows!" Kate admitted I had done her brows. "I love her!" said Kate. "It's the coolest thing that I ever discovered. My girlfriend Rita took me . . . and Rita's brows are beautiful!"

Oprah turned to Ellen and said her brows looked good too and asked if she also went to me. "Yes!" Ellen exclaimed. "I've been going to her long before Kate went." The three of them talked about me and how much they loved their eyebrows.

When I saw the show, I couldn't believe it! These very accomplished women were talking about me and complimenting my work! It was completely out of the blue and unexpected. Now, we all need affirmation to keep going, to know that we are on the right path and that we are doing a good job. It is the most incredible feeling in the world when someone praises your work without your asking for it, solely because they genuinely believe in you and what you do. It validates all the long days, sleepless nights, and the striving to master your craft. What they said meant everything to me. I never forgot it. It helped me continue to move forward. After that, brows were being talked about by women everywhere. I was being recognized as the brow expert.

Oprah had me back on the show again in 2006. This time, we filmed in the main studio. When I walked onto the stage, the lights were intensely bright. I could see the semicircle rows of stadium-style seating for the audience. There was not an empty seat in the house.

I heard Oprah's distinctive voice giving me a glowing warm welcome, introducing me as "The Queen of Brows" and that I would show the audience that having the right brow shape can lift up your whole face. She said much more, but that was all I could take in.

Oprah lay back on the large reclining chair that had been placed on the stage. Now that I knew Oprah and what to expect at this appearance, I felt relaxed on the stage. I tapped into my professional flow state immediately and quickly shaped her brows.

When I finished, Oprah said to the audience, "Would you like to see my brows?"

"Woo! Look at that brow, baby!" she said in her splendid, resonant, recognizable voice. The audience applauded. She asked the producer to flash the "before" and "after" shots of her brows on the screen.

I felt like I had put a crown on a queen. It was so beautiful. It was such a special moment.

## Miracles and Blessings

That was the Oprah seal of approval. I felt like I'd received an Academy Award, and nothing would ever be the same. It was incredible. Oprah was the biggest supporter of my career, and I will always be grateful. She would often come to the salon to have me do her brows. She would walk into the reception area in such an unassuming way, smiling at everyone. I could hear the other guests whispering, "Isn't that Oprah?!"

She told me that she would find any excuse to come to LA for meetings just so she could see me. It was the biggest compliment to me as a professional. If somebody like her trusted me and believed in what I did, I needed to believe it too. It was a powerful affirmation. Her support gave me the confidence to keep going and growing in bigger and bigger ways.

After my appearance on the show in 2006, our phones rang off the hook with requests for products. I was ready for my moment. Initially, I sold my products at the salon to customers or took orders over the phone and then sent them to the fulfillment house, as I didn't know anything about warehousing. But I realized that the fulfillment house system did not work well for me as

a smaller vendor, as customer orders had to wait in a queue behind bigger brands. This was particularly frustrating for special
or rush orders. Even before my second appearance on *The Oprah
Winfrey Show*, by 2004 I decided that I needed to open my own
warehouse and fulfillment center. My accountant was against it.
"It's a big headache. Why take on the cost and the trouble of
bookkeeping and fulfilling orders? You shouldn't do it."

My instincts—my gut—had said it was the right thing to do.
When my intuition told me something this strongly, I had to act
on it. It was not acceptable to me to disappoint my customers
with long delays, and we had to be ready to level up if and when
the time came. It was one of the best decisions I made.

In 2004, I rented a six-thousand-square-foot warehouse space
nearby in the San Fernando Valley. We kept track of our inventory in large ledgers and Excel spreadsheets. I asked Tino Stan,
my salon manager, to become the head of the warehouse center.
We worked together so well, and I needed someone skilled
who I could trust with this new operation. It was an oppor-
tune moment as my niece Luca Carp had come from Romania to
work with me. With Tino's training, she later took over as salon
manager.

They were by my side as we grew over the next two years.
So after the second Oprah show aired, in 2006, it was an all-
hands-on-deck effort. All of us worked around the clock for days,
answering phones, taking orders, packing up products to ship
out. We were excited by the viewer response. I was proud that we
were able to fulfill every request quickly with our new warehouse
set up. I was also proud that Anastasia Beverly Hills products
were getting into the hands of customers around the country.
Brows were becoming part of the everyday beauty routine.

Soon we had between twenty and twenty-five people working at the warehouse, many of them Romanians. They had been doctors, accountants, or professors in Romania but could not do those jobs in America because they did not speak English. It was such a privilege that I was in the position to give an opportunity to people in the same situation I had been when we arrived. It was very satisfying to me to pay it forward. I knew what a difference it could make in their lives. Tino spoke Romanian, so they were able to communicate with him. Byron, Tino's second-in-command, was Hispanic. As the team expanded, it became like a big Romanian and Latino family. And of course, Christopher Kraul was our computer wizard who kept our inventory and operations organized. They all worked so hard, were so dedicated and so proud to be working with us. This is how we built the business from the ground up.

## The Kindness Principle

There are certain rules I abide by in business:

Rule #1: *Always Protect Your Client.*
Rule #2: *Treat Everyone with Kindness.*

I have found that, in business as with all aspects of life, how you treat people makes all the difference in how they work and interact with your customers. You get what you give.

I always say that I learned from the best. I watched how Oprah interacted with everyone when I was on the show and the many times I saw her thereafter. She was respectful, appreciative. She was considerate of other people's time and generous with her own. She took care to compliment the people she worked with and build them up. When you are around someone like this, you understand what being humble truly means. It seemed like Oprah never forgot where she came from. This was evident when, on one of her visits to LA, Oprah introduced me to her longtime best friend, Gayle King, whom she had known since her college days. Gayle was a strong, confident, intelligent woman. I connected with her immediately. We even had the same birthday! There was something very moving to me about how honest and genuine they were with each other, as only happens with old friends who knew you *before*—when you were just dreaming of your life. There is a trust, a grounding, a feeling of being home. I was honored to witness this warmth between them, which seemed to encircle me in a big hug too.

Even though she was the biggest influencer there was, at the very top of the pyramid, she treated everyone with kindness. Kindness is such a rare, beautiful, and unexpected thing; it kind of stops you in your tracks. You can't help but want to reciprocate. I was no Oprah, but I aspired to be like her. I was resolved to be as mindful as she was in my own small way and stay grounded, humble, and kind.

It was an important lesson to hold on to now as my business was moving forward at a breathtaking pace. I had my warehouse in place. I was ready for my next moment, ready to scale up.

# The Level-Up Checklist

Every day is an opportunity to do better than the day before. Effort + Energy = Excellence.

Use this checklist to be ready to level up when the spotlight shines on you.

**Expect Excellence**
Hold yourself to your highest standards.

**Step Out of Your Comfort Zone**
Do something new that directly adds to your skills.

**Do Something Kind**
In giving, you get in return. Business and life are about relationships.

**Build a Solid Foundation**
Know what infrastructure is needed to support your dreams.

**Stay Focused**
Master your craft; everything else will come.

**Imagine Greatness**
Give yourself permission to imagine success.

CHAPTER NINE

# Mothers and Mentors
# Make the Difference

There really are places in the heart you don't
even know exist until you love a child.

—ANNE LAMOTT

There is something about being a mother that changes you, turns you inside out, teaches you things you didn't know and things you needed to learn. Anastasia Beverly Hills would not be the company it is today if I had not hired, fired, and rehired my daughter. They were some of the most difficult experiences of my life. I've mentioned it many times before, but never in much detail until now.

438 North Bedford Drive had already been a bustling place, but after my Oprah appearance the salon had become the hottest address in LA. Everyone wanted to be seen here. Paparazzi hid behind trees outside the door trying to snap the comings and goings. Celebrities waited for me next to my regular clients in the reception area. I walked through my day as usual, greeting clients with a smile on my face, my black dress and pearls perfectly groomed. I should have been feeling like I was on top of the

163

> **Even as a small child, I understood that women had secrets, and that some of these were only to be told to daughters. In this way we were bound together for eternity.**
>
> —Alice Hoffman, novelist

world. But instead, I felt only a deep sadness and anxiety that I could not push my way through. My mind was whirling, my pulse was racing. *I had just fired my own daughter.* I loved Claudia fiercely with all my being and in that softest, most tender spot inside my heart that a mother holds for her child. I hoped she still knew that. But I was afraid that she had walked away for good.

Many people have commented on how lucky I am that my daughter chose to work in my business. In the beginning it wasn't entirely her choice. I was always working, so I suggested this arrangement to keep a close eye on her, and I offered to pay her for her efforts. During her school vacations, Claudia worked part time at the reception to earn some money for her personal expenses. She proved to be extremely efficient, and it turned out to be a valuable experience for her. I must admit, I was stricter with her than I was with other employees, as I wanted to set a strong example for her. My daughter had been by my side every step of the way as Anastasia Beverly Hills came into being. The business, Claudia, and I were growing up together; the three of us were intertwined.

On that day it came to a grinding halt. We got to a breaking point that hit me between the eyes. Claudia was now working at the front desk full time. I loved having her there and our clients loved her too. She did a great job at work, but like many young people at that age, she was obsessed with her social life. I could understand that, as I had felt the same way as a teen: wearing blue eye shadow and my contraband Italian leather boots to hang out with my friends and flirt with boys.

The problem began when, after staying out with her friends, Claudia started to come in late to work in the morning. That I could not understand. Punctuality is my first rule in the salon for every employee. I believe being on time for an appointment shows respect for the client, respect for your work. She certainly knew that. She also knew an empty desk was not the reception I wanted for our clients who all counted on our top-level efficiency and service. The first time she was late, I held back my critique, trying to give her a little slack. She was still a kid, after all.

The second time she was late, the tension between us exploded. My daughter and I stood face-to-face behind closed doors in the private office at the salon like two coiled cobras. She was mad and so was I. She was defiant in the way teenagers are, and I felt angry that she was not being as professional as I thought she should be. As many parents of teenagers have experienced, it is very hard for a mom to raise a teenage daughter. It is also very difficult for a boss to manage a teenager. To do both is the ultimate challenge.

"If you come in late one more time, I am going to fire you," I said as strongly as I could. It was something that I never in my wildest dreams thought I would say to her, and something I never imagined I would actually have to do. I have since learned that as a parent I would never again threaten to do something that I wasn't emotionally prepared to follow through on. The same rule applies to business.

We stood there looking at each other, both of us slightly bent over, leaning into each other's space. I hoped that my tough words would make an impact and that she would be contrite. But instead of apologizing as I thought she would, she said nothing. I could see her thin, lithe body shaking with emotion, yet she held back. Instead, she looked me in the eye, exhaled an exasperated "humph," turned on her heel, and walked out. That was as unexpected for me as everything else that had happened.

I stayed behind, trying to cool down before opening the door to the main room and all the staff. I hoped that this was the end of it, and she had learned her lesson. I wanted to move on. But clearly she wasn't ready to do so. A few days later, she came in late again.

And so, I fired her.

Watching her leave the salon that day broke my heart and twisted my stomach upside down. I never had ulcers, but I was sure that this is what they would feel like. What had I done? Was she going to hate me now? Was our relationship irrevocably broken?

Claudia decided she would move out and live on her own, and she found a job at an insurance company. The house was unbearably quiet without her. I couldn't sleep. I paced around in my bathrobe, fearing that I had lost her for good. I sat in her room, which was still filled with most of her things and the scent of her perfume, and cried. Not even my flower garden, my usual source of peace and happiness, could give me any comfort. We had experienced small disagreements before; now we had gone from zero to nuclear. The thought of being estranged from her was excruciating. I could not talk about it with anyone for fear of that making it come true. Only my mother knew she had moved out, and that's because she lived with me.

Had I made a mistake, I wondered? I overcame so many obstacles and fears in my life, but this was an entirely new experience. I didn't know what to do or how to make it right. I had been so consumed with the business consequences of her actions, of being in the boss mindset, I realized what I was now feeling was the disconnect between my mind and heart, between boss and mom. What could I do to repair the situation? In the end, as it always does, the answer came down to love. Life and love are both four-letter words inextricably connected with each other. I had made the hard call as the business owner, but as a mom, my job was to love and provide for her. Maybe I should have approached the situation from another perspective, more like a mentor—the other kind of nurturing and guiding figure who could have coached her more effectively through the situation. I could do that, I thought, if she ever came back.

I wanted to call her to discuss everything that had happened and all that I had discovered about myself and about us. But I forced myself to be patient. I thought instead about what my daughter would actually need from me right now. How could I show her that I truly loved her? I realized that I must give her the space to sort things out for herself. I knew she had a strong work ethic. She was exceptionally talented. I hadn't found anyone as good as she was to replace her, so the job was still open, and I wanted her back desperately. But it was important for *her* to ask for her job back. The decision had to come from her.

After a long month apart, she came to me and asked to borrow money for her rent. When I saw her, I wanted to jump up and down for joy, but I didn't show it. We sat together at the kitchen table, our favorite place to talk. I knew in my bones, as mothers do, that she was not happy working at the insurance company even if she didn't say it.

"I'm sorry, I can't do that," I said. I hoped this might sway her toward coming back to Anastasia Beverly Hills, coming home. I also wanted her to learn that she could not expect things would just be given to her. It took everything I had to remain firm as I looked into her eyes, but somehow, I did it. She remained quiet. I could tell she was thinking about her options. I held my breath. I knew that it was my time to give her a nudge.

"You are very talented, Claudia. I know that you can do the work better than anyone. You can have your job back if you want it," I told her. Before she could respond, I felt that we also had to reach a professional understanding. Despite the fact that she was still very young, I felt that if she wanted to work with me, she needed to be serious about her job, to have discipline and act responsibly.

"When you walk in that front door, I am not your mother, I am your boss. I am going to be harder on you because you are an example."

Much to my relief, she accepted my terms and the job. I hugged her to me, to my heart, where she belonged. I am not sure who cried harder, me or her. We moved forward together.

Over time, Claudia worked in every department, including marketing and sales, to learn each part of the business. When she found her passion in makeup and color cosmetics, that became her business. She was in charge of it. Of course, we talked about production and development, but that part of the company was—and is—her baby. She found her own place in the industry, developed and honed her own forward-thinking marketing techniques, and did a phenomenal job. Long gone was that terrible time when I called her at eight thirty in morning and she was sleeping. Now I call her and ask her to leave work because she's there too much!

But I would never forget what happened. It was a pivotal moment for us, for me. We had reached a turning point in our relationship. Somehow, we both grew up a little bit. I could see her as the young woman she now was, instead of a girl. While I would always be her mom, at work I was her boss and mentor.

## Making Motherhood Work with Work

My experience of being a mother and working is unique because, in addition to the challenge of balancing these two spheres, my daughter works with me in the business. As I was figuring it out, my daughter was there, experiencing it with me. I realized later that she was also learning from me, which happened by proximity and through her abilities. I wanted to be an example to her of courage, resilience, and excellence and to lay the foundation for her success the way my mother did for me.

The example of my own working mother was so helpful. How she crafted her working life was a blueprint for my own approach. At a young age, I saw the world through the lens of a confident, hardworking mother who made me believe there were endless opportunities. As a girl, I spent every day with her at her shop, and she shared the disappointments and the triumphs with me. She never talked to me as if I was a child but rather as a person who could be trusted in business situations; our conversations were always about practical things. I learned from her that love is an *action*. She worked nonstop to keep us fed and safe. She didn't have the time to participate in any of my student or social activities. Her love was expressed in the action of providing for us and giving me responsibilities beyond my years, like pinning a hem or cutting a pattern or talking with her customers. It was through this work with fabric and fit that I learned about fashion, proportion, and what would look good on other women (and on me). I developed my own sense of style. Today, people often ask me who my stylist is and are surprised to hear that I don't have one!

Through these tasks, I knew my mother had an unassailable belief in my competence, which, in turn, gave me confidence. I always wanted to live up to her faith in me. I had this very same belief in my daughter. Through my experience, I learned that when your child sees you work—sees your values, your skills, your creativity—it can benefit them as well. Working at my mother's shop taught me how to interact with a variety of people, build strong relationships, listen deeply, and be curious about business and the world around me.

In Romania, I was always known as Victoria's daughter. She was as well known in Constanţa as I was later in Beverly Hills. She was the center of everything; my identity was wrapped up in hers. I left Romania because I wanted freedom, but I also wanted the chance to find out who I was as Anastasia and not just Victoria's daughter. I came here, started working, and without even knowing it, I became my mother. That is often the way it is with mothers and daughters, I am sure; one day we wake up and realize how similar we are. And see the traits that are passed down from generation to generation.

When Claudia was young, I would have her come to the salon after school. I could see her from the corner of my eye as she would do her homework. As I watched her, she was watching me too. I could see her observing and absorbing everything we did, forming her own ideas that shaped the extraordinary person she would become. Operating my own business allowed me to have different options from those who work in other ways or for other people. I was able to bring my daughter to my work and, of course, not everyone can do that. In addition, I also had family and friends who helped me in hundreds of logistical ways so that I could focus on work. I am forever grateful to all of them. I know that having support and a community of people during those young years is vital. That is why the proverb "It takes a village to raise a child" resonates so deeply with every parent.

> **Like so many working mothers all over the world, I feel the constant struggle to be the best mother I can, whilst setting a good example to my children to work hard. I travel for work when it's necessary, and I miss them all the time when I am away.**
>
> —Victoria Beckham

Even though I was doing the best I could in my work, to do better in my craft and to provide the best life I could for my child, sometimes I wondered: *Was I making the right decisions? Would something I did or didn't do today affect my daughter's long-term happiness or impact my work in an unforeseen way?* I am sure that you have felt the same way if you are a working parent. When you are at work, you are also thinking about your child. When you are at home, you are thinking about work issues.

I talked about that struggle with everyone I knew—my clients, my employees, my friends who chose to be full-time parents at home. Working parents were all around me: the CEOs of the biggest companies, the most beautiful models, the most talented actresses, the most famous hairstylists and makeup artists. I found that I was doing the same mental gymnastics—the should haves, would haves, could haves—that twirled in every mother's mind and kept her up at night.

No matter the circumstances—CEO, celebrity, business professional, or stay-at-home mom—all the women I knew were working hard. *Every mom is a working mom, whether she runs the home or runs a business.* I think that mothers who manage their households like CEOs are superhumans. They overcome challenges—physical, psychological, fiscal, and more—often without any formal training in those areas, yet they find ways to navigate daily obstacles with determination and resilience. The hours invested in raising their children shape them into remarkable individuals who eventually contribute positively to society. Life, work, and parenting is messy. There is no perfect way to do it. You have to find your own way. One secret all the working moms I knew had in common for creating calm in the chaos between work and parenting was to focus 100 percent on the matter at hand—whether work, a task, or their child. At home, it didn't need to be a grand gesture. If they were at the dinner table: no phone, no email. Cooking meals or folding laundry together was a perfect time to check in with their child and ask how they were doing, how can I help, and to talk about life and share the bigger picture of why they needed to work, travel, do art, or spend time away from their child.

I also adopted this in my life too. For Claudia and me, Sunday became our time. I loved Sundays. The best memories from my own childhood were when my loud, big, close-knit Macedonian family would gather every Sunday to cook, talk, cry, and laugh together around the kitchen table. On Sundays, I would cook her favorite chicken dish and give my attention to my daughter, my mom, and sometimes friends. I tried not to talk about business, though we still did, as it was our lives. It was very important to me to spend this time with Claudia. Finding those special moments with each other, making family traditions, kept my daughter and I close during her childhood years, and still does.

> **When I was doing something I was told was a 'two-man job' but in fact it turned out to be a one-woman job, I called my mom to say thank you for teaching me how to do literally everything . . . when I was a kid and she was a single mom figuring out how to run a business and send two kids to school.**
>
> —Sarah Brown, former beauty director of *Vogue*

I think that when kids understand why their mother works, they don't feel resentful; they instead even become more helpful. When they grow up, they will be hardworking too, because they know how hard you worked. I often see this cycle with immigrant families, although of course, it is not limited to them. The second generation, seeing their parents' sacrifices and hard work, strives to honor their elders by working even harder to reach new heights of achievement. I believe if your child sees you working hard, developing your skills and passions (whatever form that takes for you), it models a way for them to envision their future.

It comes down to deciding how to make all aspects of your work and life function best for you. Every choice, whether it is going to a job, managing a household as a stay-at-home mom, not having children, or mothering by being a mentor, has its own challenges, gains, and losses. I don't think we have to do it like anyone else, but we do need to be OK in living with what we choose.

I chose to make my business my priority and to share that with my child. Just like my mother, my work is my passion. It is what I do and who I am. Everything I do is work oriented. Even if I go to dinner, I'm in work mode. Of course, I have dinners with my friends, I cook, and I relax. But it's something that's constant.

If someone asks me what my hobby is, my answer would be "work." Even when I am at work, I don't feel like I am working because I love it. I never think, *Oh, I have to go to work. I can't wait for it to be done.* I wake up every day and say to myself, "I have to go to work! I'm so excited. I have a purpose today and I'm going to do what I love, and I am going to share that with others." My life is my work, and my work is my life. So to me it doesn't feel like work, it is my *lifestyle*. I think that's the key in life.

It has come full circle in my family: Grandmother, mother, myself, and my daughter all have this same work ethic and passion. When I think about it now, if it all ended for me tomorrow, I would say my greatest achievement in life, even beyond the business I built, is that my daughter has found her purpose. And that she does it extraordinarily well.

Raising a child takes a tremendous amount of work. That's

why I always say that every mom is a working mom, whether or not they have a paid job. When a paid job or career is layered onto these responsibilities, finding your balance as a working mother can take time. No one teaches you how to make motherhood compatible with work. I believe the answer to how to do it is so very personal and individual. Life isn't one-size-fits-all. My way of doing it may not be yours. I offer it in the hope that there is something in my story that might be useful to you, just as I have learned from other women about how they blended parenting, work, and relationships in an artful way to shape their life. I think the way we figure it out is by doing what we women do best—wrap our arms around those we love, those who need our gifts, and learn from each other's stories.

## Your Magic Makes the Difference

Working with so many women of all kinds over the years, I have learned that whether you are a mother or not, women are wonderful nurturers, exhibiting a mom-like energy fueled by love, protection, and generosity. Whether it is innate or conditioned, we are excellent at caring in so many different ways. Through sharing their skills, knowledge, wisdom, mastery, contacts, or time, women are good at teaching and nurturing people's character, confidence, talents, and dreams. Every mother, in every time and place, has had to find her own way to mom and to mentor. Whether you are a mother, an aunt, a sister, or an executive, or you spend your time nurturing trainees or coworkers, volunteering, or caregiving, I bet that *mom energy* flows from your soul into the world in some way. I nurture my daughter, but I also nurture other women and people in my life. We each have some-thing special to give, big or small, influenced by where we come from and the choices we have made. Sometimes just the *belief* that someone *can* succeed is the magic that makes the difference. Women are good at instilling this belief in each other, and in the next generation. For me, supporting and mentoring other women and entrepreneurs is my passion and purpose. When I finally gained the resources and the ability to help young people in struggling circumstances work in the beauty field and build a better life for themselves, there was no way I could stand on the sidelines.

When I was growing up under one of the harshest Communist regimes there had ever been, everyone was afraid all the time. People put their compassion and their dreams on hold to scrape by and to survive. It was impossible for me to look away from the suffering around me and particularly from the eyes of hungry children who had no means to escape. Every child is so special—who knows what great talents never got to be expressed in that time, in that place. I was a child then myself, but I think my soul was already mothering the greatness I could see in others.

I was trained by my family to put fear aside and to summon up my strength, grit, and perseverance to endure. I watched my aunts and my mother work really, really hard and do what they had to do for their kids, managing the household and providing for the future. I think most immigrants whose families endured hardships have a similar story. My grandmother raised her seven children while also running a twenty-acre farm—the animals and the crops—and she managed it all entirely on her own when my grandfather was in the war. The memory of her strength and presence, barely five feet tall with her dark braided hair always covered under a thick black scarf called a *dada*, always stayed with me. My grandparents had been immigrants themselves to Romania. They struggled every day to make their way in a different culture where they didn't know the ways or the language. I felt as if their immigrant experience as well as their scrappy spirit was seared into my DNA and mirrored in my own journey.

When I came to this country not speaking the language, being new, I felt like it was the same. I still had to find a way to survive. There were times when I was frightened. I had to put any fear quickly aside and be brave and resourceful. I was a single mother, an immigrant, with no other financial support, no safety net. Finding work was my goal. Perfecting my artistry was important to my soul, of course. But my top priority was to provide a home, food, and necessities for my daughter, myself, and my mother. I didn't have a road map or a giant master plan. I was just trying to figure it out one step at a time as the path opened in front of me.

# Life operates on the principle that what we put in is what we get out.

My friend Patrick, a very wise elder I know, told me a beautiful story that stuck with me. Each of us is born with a magical bag we carry with us throughout our lives that collects all our experiences, good and bad, from everyone we meet: parents, siblings, friends, coworkers, bosses, and others. Eventually the bag gets very heavy. We get weighed down by carrying it. Some people just keep going, their noses to the grindstone. It is only when we finally decide to stop, look inside, and choose what to keep or discard that we can live the life we truly want.

With some success behind me, I felt that I could finally take a minute to breathe, to reflect. I took the opportunity to look inside my bag and examine what was there. I began to unload the things that I still carried from the past that needed to be discarded. I invited in what I truly wanted, which was to teach others my craft and nurture young artists, and what I had long dreamed of doing since my past in Romania, which was to help young people build a better life for themselves. I wanted to use every bit of my *mom energy* as a mother and a mentor. When you mother your child, you summon an outpouring of the highest form of love, protection, and nurturing from the very source of your being. When you mentor a young person, you offer your experience and knowledge, and you teach them skills and confidence to help them grow.

## Teaching Brows and Business

I know that I didn't build my career on talent and willpower alone. I had supporters who believed in me, which is what every young person deserves and needs but not all have. I set out to develop scholarships to beauty school for young people who wanted to gain the skills and saw beauty as a career. I also wanted to work directly with young people who could truly benefit from the focused attention of a personal apprenticeship.

Everyone needs someone
who believes in their
greatness in order to
believe in it themselves.

I created the Anastasia Brighter Horizon Foundation in 2013 to underwrite, with the help of my clients and friends, the scholarship program, and we aligned with the Paul Mitchell Beauty School. I was also introduced to Carla Palmer at United Friends of the Children (UFC), an agency that helps current and former foster youth with transitional housing and education. Carla was a counselor at the time and later director of development at the UFC.

I made an appointment to meet her at her office. I think I loved Carla the minute we met, and she later told me the feeling was mutual. When we talked, she felt she could see my heart. And I could see hers. Carla has that sort of big spirit that lifts you up, embraces you, and makes you feel that everything is OK. This made her perfect for her job. Not only was she beautiful, energetic, and dedicated to service, but she took a deep interest in and knew the circumstances of all the young people she worked with. For so many, foster care meant being forgotten. After aging out of that system, the UFC was often a lifeline for them. I hoped I could be another.

Over the next couple of months, Carla and I met with candidates and decided on three extraordinary young women from the program: Jessyka Hill, Arroya Shepherd, and Lasandra Joseph. They reminded me of myself back at the beginning when I had applied for the job at the Giovanna-Jutta salon. I could see each had the same sort of determination that had pushed me forward. I told Carla that we would help these girls get through the beauty school training and tackle the coursework. Each would be paired with a personal mentor from the salon, a brow specialist. They would apprentice with me as well.

When I brought these young women to the salon, I was hoping that we would be inspiring to them. What I found instead was that they were inspiring to us. Everyone who worked at the salon was impressed by the strong desire each of them had to learn the business and to succeed. Even our clients took an interest in them. Lasandra was a big fan of Kim Kardashian, and Kim helped me create a surprise for her.

One day I said to Lasandra, "You never know what's going to happen today. You never know what life will bring you!" She nodded, gave me a brief smile, and kept looking down at her work. That's when Kim, who had been waiting in the hallway, came through the door, holding a special card for her. Lasandra turned around and looked at Kim, her eyes wide. She lost all her words, let out a little "Whoop!" and hugged her. It was such a wonderful moment for all of us! I felt so much joy in being able to make a positive difference in their lives.

Something magical happens when you give to others; the same is true when you mother, when you mentor. Each generates an incredible feeling that is better than anything you could bottle or buy. I thought that I was teaching these young women about brows and business, and in the end, they were showing us how much can be accomplished through hard work, belief, and of course good brows. They graduated from beauty school and they remain each other's strong circle of support.

Being a mentor to these young women and others has given me such a sense of fulfillment. I feel grateful to be able to share my success and pay it forward. When you help other people on their climb to achievement, you get back as much joy as you give. While you are chasing your goals with determination, don't forget to look for opportunities to help nurture, mother, and support others. Being a supportive colleague, friend, or mentor even before you've made it to the pinnacle is not only fulfilling; it builds the network that gives your life meaning and purpose.

# Oscar Moment

## The United Friends of the Children Brass Ring Award

It was a beautiful, clear night in LA. The lights of Hollywood sparkled. I stood on the stage at the United Friends of the Children Gala held at Skirball Cultural Center and looked out at the packed ballroom. My daughter, Claudia, was at the table reserved for Anastasia Beverly Hills' friends. Everyone was beautifully dressed in their cocktail best. I was just presented with their highest honor, their Brass Ring Award, acknowledging my mentorship of Jessyka Hill, Arroya Shepherd, and Lasandra Joseph. It was a special moment. As an immigrant who had faced my own struggles, to be able to help these young women rise to become empowered, successful professionals was more than a dream come true. It was the completion of a journey toward service that began in my own childhood in Romania. Carla Palmer, the director of development, changed all our lives by connecting us. I looked at the faces of these three remarkable young women who overcame any challenge with resilience and determination, and I was filled with admiration. I dedicated the award to them; after all, it was their work, their openness, that allowed me into this beautiful circle of trust. That each of them is now a successful entrepreneur is another testament to the transformational power of this industry, and the ability we have to choose our own lives. Helping other people to succeed is the real magic in life.

# CHAPTER TEN

# A Passion for Innovation

Innovation is taking two things that exist
and putting them together in a new way.

—Tom Freston, cofounder of MTV

Nordstrom already had a well-established reputation as a high-end beauty destination when Dale Crichton, executive vice president of beauty, and her colleagues Debbi Hartley-Triesch and Peggy Moore came to meet me in LA. It was 2000. They had heard the buzz about my work through beauty industry circles and my media interviews and wanted to see the salon for themselves. I walked out to the reception area to find these very poised, smartly dressed women. Each was beautifully made up in an understated way, but still glamorous. They exuded a professional and sophisticated confidence that instantly drew me in. Over lunch at a nearby Beverly Hills restaurant (a rarity for me to be away from the salon), our conversation flowed easily. We realized that we had much in common, including our desire to help women look and feel their best. They invited me to present Anastasia Beverly Hills to their buying team. Of course, I immediately said

183

yes. I was ready to take our next step with Anastasia Beverly Hills, and Nordstrom was legendary for its dedication to customer experience and continuing innovation. Nordstrom's customer-first focus and commitment to excellence were aligned with my own values. I felt we had the potential for a perfect partnership. We would soon bring our products to new customers with a retail partner that shared our values.

We were on the cusp of a new beginning. We would later go on to have many game-changing partnerships with major retailers around the globe, including industry innovators Sephora and Ulta Beauty. But it was Nordstrom that opened the door to retail for us. They were our first and, as it is with most first loves, they hold a special place in our history. Our experiences with Nordstrom paved the pathway toward those other possibilities. Now, we were at the start of the next part of our growth journey.

## Bring Your Own Magic Wherever You Go

A few months after Dale and Debbi visited the salon, I flew to Nordstrom's buying offices in Seattle to introduce their team to our brow kit. Sunlight accompanied the plane as we jetted up the coast from LA. The opportunity ahead seemed to shine just as brightly. I could barely contain my excitement. It was a big deal to be invited to audition for the retail "big leagues," to see the possibility that our products would find their place on national department store counters.

Most young brands in our position would have been happy to work with Nordstrom under any terms offered. I was thrilled to be standing on the threshold of this potential partnership. We had worked hard to get to this moment. I also had a big vision for the future, and I needed to stay focused. There are times as an entrepreneur or leader when you feel truly excited and passionate about an opportunity that comes your way. I also knew that it was important not to lose sight of what I wanted in the long term and to evaluate all my options as dispassionately as possible. Dazzle can deter anyone from thinking things through. Every time I faced an opportunity such as this, I would turn it over in my mind. *Does it align with my dreams and purpose? Does this person/company/ organization operate with integrity? Am I properly set up for this expansion? Is this the right way to move forward?* The best strategy for me was to keep my feet on the ground while my head was busy thinking about my destiny. Be ready to seize an opportunity, but also be ready to walk away if it wasn't the right move.

In the case of Nordstrom, I was willing to go big or go home. I didn't yet know the Nordstrom customer, but I knew mine. I knew that most women were still learning about brows and still asking questions like "What part of my brow should I tweeze? How do I put powder on my brow? Can I make my face look like Cindy Crawford's or Jennifer Aniston's?" The key was education. I didn't want Nordstrom to just display my products on a counter, in a sea of counters competing with the impulse buys of lipsticks and lotions. I knew that my products needed a hands-on touch. Customers needed to understand the principle of the ABH Golden Ratio Shaping Technique based on their own facial bone structure and natural eyebrow shape, and they needed to learn how to use the products. Once someone experienced the beauty metamorphosis that occurs with the right brow shape, I believed they would become a lifelong customer. My focus was on delivering exceptional results for each client, knowing they would share their experiences with family and friends—person-to-person, the best advertising any brand can have. I wanted Nordstrom to offer our brow services along with our products. I also wanted to train the estheticians who would be working with the customers. Just because the industry did things in a certain way before didn't mean it couldn't do something else. I needed the partnership to make sense for my brand. I thought outside the box and wanted to do something different.

That day in Seattle, I would be one among many "new vendor" meetings hosted by Nordstrom executives. I had my one-hour slot, and I knew we had to stand out. I walked into the conference room where there was a large rectangular black table surrounded by numerous high-backed chairs. In the middle of the table was a tray of fruits and cookies, coffee, teas, and other beverages. There were fourteen people, mostly women, who greeted us, including Peggy Moore, the national merchandise manager, who would become very influential in our development at Nordstrom. I shook hands with each and then everyone sat down. All eyes turned to me.

I was ready. I had come prepared for this moment. In meetings like this, I always follow my Rule #3: *Build Relationships.* I know this to be a business truth: Selling is about conversation. The best way to sell is by engaging and connecting with your audience. I handed each person one of our brow kits and invited them to touch the five components: Tactile sensations always bring us back to childhood and play. While they were feeling their way around the kit, I asked questions. I did not focus on dollars or statistics but rather: *What made their customers excited? What did the beauty team aspire to do for their department over the next few years? How did they reach, teach, and touch their cus-*

*tomers?* Then I shared why I wanted to bring the Anastasia Beverly Hills brow service to Nordstrom.

"First of all, it is important to teach our customers how to do their brows, because most don't know what to do or what kind of transformation this technique creates," I said. "Second, if the service is done in the Nordstrom beauty department, rather than at a salon, you will have this customer coming back every three weeks. This builds connection to the store.

"On top of that," I added, "we know that we women just can't resist looking at all the counters. Even though the customer is coming in for brow service, she is likely to grab a lipstick or an eye pencil too. So, every sales employee in the department has a new opportunity to reach this customer."

I looked around the room. I could see that there were smiles, but they were not yet persuaded.

"Let me show you," I said. *This is how the magic happens. It is always in the doing.* I had noticed the woman sitting opposite from me had eyebrows that were so light you could hardly see them.

"May I demonstrate on you?" I asked her. She nodded her permission. I got up and stood next to her. I purposely positioned her chair with her face in full view of everyone around the table so they could all watch as I worked on her. I wanted them to see how easy my brow shaping technique was. I opened the kit and took out the stencil that would work best for her facial structure and eyebrow shape. I did her left brow in two minutes, leaving the other as it was. The difference was dramatic. There were literal gasps.

"Wow," said one buyer. "How did you do that?!"

With that one eyebrow, I proved my whole premise about the need for a brow service and the amazing results that customers would experience. The buyers looked around the room at each other in delight. I knew we had a match even before I completed her second brow.

Destiny has its own timeline. I was the right person, with the right product, at the right time. Peggy Moore shared with me later that Nordstrom had already been in the process of expanding their beauty categories and developing makeup artist brands like Trish McEvoy and Bobbi Brown. They were looking for new brands that could set them apart from other department stores and had already started to think about adding services. It seemed that Anastasia Beverly Hills would fit with their artistry lines, and we would give Nordstrom an industry first, as no one had done brows before. Nordstrom would also level up their customer experience by offering a boutique salon service in their stores.

Nordstrom embraced my vision. I knew we were going to do something innovative and extraordinary together. The intent was to bring a little piece of Anastasia Beverly Hills into the Nordstrom environment with my trained estheticians. Debbi Hartley-Triesch, who is now the executive vice president and general merchandise manager of beauty, accessories, and home at Nordstrom, later shared their thinking with me: If you could not go to Beverly Hills, we would bring Beverly Hills to you right in your local Nordstrom.

## Build an Army of Salespeople

I was about to step onto a whole new stage under a bright spotlight. We launched in 2000, at the dawn of a whole new century, with twenty stores. I was exhilarated. I was ready. We were finally going to be able to bring more beauty to the lives of women around the country, accomplishing a dream I had since we created our first products. Now the only thing left to do was to execute and make magic happen. I hired my friend Desiree Gruber, who owned Full Picture, a PR and marketing firm, to promote the products.

From the outset, quality had been my top priority. I aimed to provide the best products while educating my clients on how to use them effectively for optimal results, emphasizing that their unique features require personalized brow solutions. I believed 100 precent that my products and my groundbreaking methodologies would make a difference to them. I didn't want to just make a sale. It was of paramount importance to me that we help the client or customer select the *right* product for her that she would use and love, so that she could walk away feeling good about herself. I wanted to train the sales team to have this same approach at every counter, everywhere.

To be able to go as far and as wide and as *big* as I truly wanted, I knew that we had to take our selling and marketing to a whole new level and build an *army* of salespeople. It would include estheticians for the Nordstrom counters who we trained in the ABH Golden Ratio Shaping Technique and dedication to customer service. I also dreamed that this network would eventually extend to the everyday woman who would learn and then rave about Anastasia Beverly Hills products and our service with the people in her life. Before there was Instagram, TikTok, and 24/7 streaming media, communication happened person-to-person. Women are happy to share information and inspiration with each other. I wanted to tap into that natural flow that occurs friend-to-friend,

> **There are many things you can do overnight ... but there is no such thing as an overnight success.**
>
> —Tory Burch,
> fashion designer

mother-to-daughter, sister-to-sister. The partnership with Nordstrom was our opportunity to build this network. It would take a huge, co-ordinated effort to launch.

The whole home office team—as well as our product development teams and those in the warehouse—rolled up their sleeves to support our rollout. Not only did we need to produce more product, but we also needed logistics for distribution and tools for training local estheticians. Our Nordstrom counterparts, Peggy and Debbi, and the teams at every location got sucked in too. They put their arms around me like I was a precious gem. They mentored me but also gave me the space and support to fulfill my vision, expand the product line, and get trained people into the store to work with customers. I will always be grateful for their long-term approach to business, which allowed my brand the time to find its place.

It was a slow, methodical development, with some early learnings. The first brow services were offered in rooms "off the floor." People could sign up at the counter and be escorted to the room. Women were used to just browsing the cosmetics department for products. They didn't understand that they were able to sign up for a service. They were hesitant to leave their shopping routine to go to another space.

Always ready to innovate and to pivot, Nordstrom designed a space next to the counter, with screens around it for privacy. This location made all the difference. People started to sign up for services and experience the transformative ABH Golden Ratio Shaping Technique. I was not going to leave anything to chance. I went to every store myself to work with our estheticians and our customers. Claudia and I spent nearly every weekend on the road at a Nordstrom, or alternatively at industry conventions or trade shows. We worked all week in the salon and then traveled to different cities by plane or car, living out of our suitcases to work with customers. It was our way of life for many years. We were stylish vagabonds in makeup and high heels.

Sometimes I felt bad about the intensity of it all. Claudia was just a young woman but was living the lifestyle of a career-driven forty-year-old—working all the time with no vacations. It was physically hard, but we had the stamina and energy to do it. The truth was that we both loved it. We were sharing our passion with each other and everyone we encountered.

When I did personal appearances at a Nordstrom store, whether for a day or for a weekend, the Nordstrom teams would switch around the beauty department floor to accommodate more shoppers and curious browsers. They would place several service booths (chairs with privacy screens around the sides and back) next to the central elevators so that the public would have a good view. There would be spotlights and music. It was like a big party inside Nordstrom. I would work continuously, morning to night, as I usually do, enjoying meeting and spending time with my customers. Crowds formed around the elevators. People lined up. Nordstrom employees directed the flow. To keep the line moving, Claudia or local estheticians would sometimes start serving the customer with color or product advice, but I would always do the brows of each and every person. It was electric. We were surrounded by a buzz of excitement as all the women in line would be talking to each other. Friends would tell friends. I had happy customers and happy partners. My methodology and products were becoming more well-known. I was in my element bringing beauty to women's lives, one eyebrow at a time.

## Customer Obsessed

Several times a year, Nordstrom would host an in-store event called the Beauty Trend Show, a kind of fashion show through the lens of beauty. They were always looking for new ways to give value to customers and enhance their experience. I loved to participate in their events. People would line up outside in the early morning before department store doors opened. Events usually started around 8:00 a.m., and customers would arrive as early as 6:00 a.m. to get in line. There would be crowds of five-hundred-plus women drinking their coffee, waiting to hear the latest trends and see demonstrations.

Nordstrom had a tradition that all the salespeople working that day would stand in front of the doors when they opened in the morning to greet the customers with applause and thank them for shopping there. It was part of the Nordstrom philosophy of creating a welcoming environment for consumers, which included their employees as well. If you walked into the employee entrance behind the department sales floors, as I sometimes did, they were clean, nicely decorated spaces. The company would regularly recognize employee achievements. All of this contributed to an atmosphere brimming with activity, excitement, and growth.

When Nordstrom opened their new store in Chicago on Michigan Avenue, I received what I felt was my own recognition of achievement when they chose our brand to be one of the anchor vendors in the new store. Located among the luxury stores on the street dubbed the Magnificent Mile, similar to Rodeo Drive in LA or New York's Fifth Avenue, this was a huge new venture in a major market. I was thrilled that they selected Anastasia Beverly Hills to be a part of its launch.

I flew in from the warmth of Los Angeles to be greeted at O'Hare airport by the cold winter weather. It was snowing, and ice crackled on the ground as I walked. There was a glittering party the night before the opening hosted by Nordstrom executives and attended by many of Chicago's local socialites and luminaries. The next day at the store, hundreds of women browsed the beauty department and patiently waited on lines to see me. I was concentrating on a customer when someone came up behind me and wrapped me up in a big hug, loudly saying my name. The warm voice was unmistakable. It was *Oprah*! She had heard that I was in Chicago, and she decided to come to Nordstrom to see me. Needless to say, her presence caused pandemonium. Even though she was often spotted around town, as her Harpo Studios was based in Chicago, this spontaneous appearance in the middle of a department store was an unexpected special occasion. It was a first for Nordstrom and added a sprinkle of stardust to the new location, becoming part of its folklore—shoppers always glancing around, looking from the corners of their eyes as they browsed the counters in the hope of another "Oprah spotting."

It took me a few moments to truly absorb that she was there standing right next to me. I was so incredibly moved by her personal support I could barely squeak out a hello. But, as I have come to know, that is the kind of person she is: caring and generous with her time and attention. We chatted together for a while, and she talked to a few of the customers who were lined up patiently waiting for their turn with me, telling them that I did *her* brows too. It was another Oscar moment with Oprah. How could I feel that it was anything else but extraordinary? The most influential person on television at the time had come to see me—the immigrant who had arrived in the country without a penny to her name. It was truly a testament to the power of hard work and believing in yourself, proof that dreams could come true in America.

## The Downside to Up

The challenge of growing our business to meet the new consumer demand was very exciting, but the reality of accomplishing our goals wasn't always rosy or glamorous. While I had the backing of my teams and my partners, I still had to figure things out for myself. I made the mistake that many young entrepreneurs make— I tried to expand my product line too quickly. I decided that we should launch a body care line. Body care products were getting a lot of traction in the industry at the time, with many brands entering the market. Back then, we were only at the dawn of this revolution. Organic foods were just taking hold of the culture. *Natural* was the word of the day. The concept of natural was very appealing to me, and I thought that my customers would feel the same way. We created a new line of luxury body care products to sell in Nordstrom. They were made of pure shea butter, packaged in little glass jars using only natural preservatives. All went well in the beginning. But the products did not have a long shelf life. There are great challenges in producing cosmetic products: ingredients, regulations, shelf life, and also technology. You may be able to dream it, but you need chemists and manufacturers to be able to produce what you envision in a way that is actually usable to consumers. In this case, what I wanted to do just couldn't be executed well at that time. It is hard to accept this kind of letdown, emotionally and financially, but I have learned it is part of business and life. Not everything works. Some things fail spectacularly.

> ## An entrepreneur must react quickly and decisively, putting the well-being of customers first.

> " You have to be able to pivot when you find out what the realities are, because the world changes by the minute and you have to be flexible too. If you don't have the ability to pivot, you're going to go to zero.
>
> —Kevin O'Leary, *Shark Tank*'s Mr. Wonderful "

We took all the body care products back from the stores. In addition, thousands of units in the warehouse had to be sent to a facility to be destroyed. We had to pay for all of that. In the end, we went back to our core products. It cost tens of thousands of dollars, which had an impact on our still small-sized business.

Fortunately, we were able to survive. Sometimes a concept, brand extension, or product is just not right for your business. I had to accept that this was not the path I was destined to walk—at least, not yet.

## Imagine. Believe. Achieve. Repeat.

A business must always be in motion, building and rebuilding, in order to thrive. This is the way of all things in nature and the cosmos. I felt this too; the need to be constantly innovating, improving, and pushing ahead—despite setbacks and even successes. I've always sought ways to improve our products using new technologies. Sometimes a product or an idea is just ahead of its time. For instance, when we launched our brow pomade in 2000, which I had previously made in the small batches that were much loved by my salon clients, it was not waterproof. It would take more than a decade for the technology to catch up to my product needs. When that technology became available, we revisited and reinvented. We relaunched our brow pomade in 2014 with a new waterproof formula. It remains one of our bestselling products. Keeping an eye on trends, like the soap brow and laminated look, inspired us to introduce Brow Freeze Gel. And when COVID kept people at home, our response was to develop the Anastasia Beverly Hills Brow App, brow shaping advice virtually on-demand—an industry first. A customer could upload a picture of themselves and then play with different brow stencils on their face in real time. The app showed how to use the golden ratio to select their brow shape and order the right products to create it.

The need for innovation, product, and process improvement never stops. I will never rest on five-star reviews or beauty awards from last year. We keep imagining, reimagining, and improving in an ever-expanding cycle of growth.

> " The biggest thing that kills [a business] is complacency. . . . You always want to be on the move when you've got a great business. . . . The belief that tomorrow is more exciting than today [needs] to permeate the organization.
>
> —Warren Buffett "

## The Expanding Beauty Scene

The retail environment is always in motion too, continually shifting the shopping experience. By the early 2000s it was changing rapidly, led by Sephora, which revolutionized the beauty business. A retailer that exclusively focused on beauty, Sephora had burst onto the American scene with an innovative new merchandising concept presenting prestige cosmetics in open-sell displays instead of behind the beauty counter. Customers could reach for products and try them on before buying, inviting them to interact and play with the transformational magic of makeup. This strategy captured the imagination of beauty enthusiasts, and Sephora quickly became a shopping destination.

In 2004, Margarita Arriagada, Sephora's then-head of color cosmetics and later chief merchant, invited me to have lunch with her in Beverly Hills. A very attractive woman with long dark hair and a warm, wide-open smile, she was passionate, experienced, and confident. Somewhere between our entrée and coffee, Margarita told me that she wanted to bring Anastasia Beverly Hills to Sephora.

Of course, at first I was thrilled! I knew that being in Sephora would allow us to reach even more women and make them feel beautiful. Still, I hesitated. I usually said yes immediately to opportunities, but this would be a big shift for us to transition from our core counter-based brow service concept that we had at Nordstrom to Sephora's open-sell environment. Margarita was persistent, and after a few months, we found a way forward together. I accepted and never looked back.

One of our first events at Sephora was at their high-profile location in Times Square. It was a scene right out of the movies. Outside was the noise and bustle of the famous street, and inside, a sprawling line of people waiting to meet me and to sit in Sephora's signature black chairs for demonstrations. It was a successful start that set the stage for many in-store events to come and the strong, productive relationship that continues to this day. At the helm of Sephora North America is CEO Artemis Patrick, who has been an invaluable partner to Anastasia Beverly Hills. Artemis's dedication to Sephora's core values of innovation and artistry has continually inspired Claudia and me, as well as the entire team at Anastasia Beverly Hills.

Ulta Beauty, another innovator in the beauty space, was also making its mark at this time, quickly expanding its retail doors across the US. In 2008, we began our long-standing partnership with them, extending our reach to even more people around the country. We continued to have our Nordstrom business with our trained brow estheticians as well as our Beverly Hills salon, but in Sephora and Ulta Beauty our displays would become our new storefront. They would represent who we were, what we stood for, and the quality of our products to current fans and to anyone else who might try us out for the first time. And we continued to grow our presence in US department stores, launching the brow line in Dillard's in 2011 and in Macy's in 2014. Macy's was first to launch the color line in 2015. Claudia was on hand for that first launch event—the products completely sold out even before they were finished stacking the counters.

We are also in prestige department stores globally, including Harrods and Selfridges (in the UK), Douglas (Germany, Netherlands, Austria, Spain, Poland, Switzerland, Belgium), ICI Paris XL (Netherlands, Belgium, Luxembourg), and other well-known retailers such as Boots.

For me, everything we do always comes back to my clients and customers and to making products that solve problems and offer solutions to help them feel their best. Paying attention to their needs and wishes is what shaped my business and created our success. And now, waiting in the wings, there was new digital technology that would transform how we would communicate, share information and aspiration with them, and make our brand visible around the globe.

# Anastasia's Meeting Mindset Prep

Whether you are a CEO, a manager, or an entry-level employee, you will have to present your ideas, vision, accomplishments, or products to others. Here are my rituals to prepare my thinking before a big meeting to make the most of every opportunity.

**Start-the-Day Rituals:** Every morning, I start with a brief meditation to clear my mind and set my intentions for the day. I follow this with some light exercise, which energizes me and enhances my focus. I take time to prioritize my tasks with big goals in mind, ensuring my daily actions are aligned with my long-term vision.

**Boosting Confidence Before a Big Meeting:** I prepare by researching the meeting participants and rehearsing my key points. I also visualize a positive outcome. This combination of preparation and positive visualization helps me approach the meeting with confidence.

**North Star in Decision-Making:** My North Star is always the impact on our customers and how our decisions align with our brand values. I strive to ensure that every choice enhances the customer experience.

**Combating a "No":** When I encounter a "no," I see it as an opportunity for growth rather than a setback. I ask for feedback, which helps me refine my approach. I can then pivot and find alternative solutions or opportunities.

**Wind-Down Ritual:** In the evenings, I reflect on the day, noting what went well and what I can improve. This helps me decompress and prepare for the next day with a clear mind.

# CHAPTER ELEVEN

# Without Risk There Is No Growth

Don't spend time beating on a wall,
hoping to transform it into a door.

—Coco Chanel

The year 2012 was predicted by the ancient Mayan calendar to usher in a time of cosmic change, a reset for planet Earth. Everyone waited for the unfolding to happen; books, movies, and headlines were written about it. While the year turned out to be uneventful for most, for me and our business, the prophecy of a giant shift came true. In 2012, Claudia walked into my office with an idea that would radically expand our interactions with customers and take our business into the stratosphere.

"I think we should create an Anastasia Beverly Hills channel on Instagram," she said.

She sat down in the chair in front of my desk at our new corporate headquarters. My office was decorated in the same elegant, understated pink, beige, and gold as I had decorated the salon. Claudia's long hair, which was blue at the time, was pulled back from her face, tied up on top of her head in a high ponytail.

She often pulled it back in this way when she was concentrating intensely. With her focus now on developing makeup, Claudia could be found day and night in the cosmetics lab with chemists. She was also spending hours on the emerging platform called Instagram, experimenting with and learning everything about the capabilities of digital media.

I sat down in the chair next to her. I felt the sunshine on my back from the window behind me giving everything a golden glow. She showed me the Instagram app on her iPhone. At that time, Instagram was a mere hint of the glossy, spectacular conversation hub it would become. It was where people posted interesting, beautiful, sometimes edgy pictures. She held the phone between us as colorful pictures swiped by under her blue-painted fingertips. I had never seen anything like this before. As she shared her vision for Instagram, I could feel my own excitement building. The new visual medium was in perfect synergy with our visual brand. Claudia foresaw the platform's potential as a canvas for style and artistry. We would introduce Anastasia Beverly Hills to the growing community of professionals and beauty enthusiasts on the platform, who were genuinely interested in makeup. She saw it as a place to show our products and share our application techniques and industry insider tips through tutorials and makeup transformations. She also imagined it as a place where we could support beauty professionals and up-and-coming makeup artists—a passion for both of us that had emerged from going to so many industry events.

Claudia had a definite point of view on aesthetics. As an artist and designer, I could easily imagine the architecture and design she described. We could post gorgeous, stylized photographs, professionally shot. They would be cutting-edge, inspirational, aspirational. They would be diverse images of people who loved makeup. An invitation to everyone, everywhere—from Bedford Street to Main Street—into the artistry, the vision, and the glamorous world of Anastasia Beverly Hills. We always said that *brows are a lifestyle, not just a trend.* The imagery felt so right. It captured the high style and sparkle of the Beverly Hills dream that called to me long ago from far away. The dream that still called to me.

"We would be the first," she said finally, saving this decisive part of her strategy for last. "No established beauty brand has done this before." We looked at each other.

"So, what do you think?" she asked.

## Taking It to the Next Level

When I immigrated from Romania to America, I had never thought that I would become the CEO of my own cosmetics company or build a global brand. To be honest, it wasn't in my mind at all. In many ways, I am what might be called an unexpected entrepreneur. I took my first job at Giovanna-Jutta because I had to pay the bills. I saw a need for brows that I could fill, and I liked to be challenged; that's my personality. As my passion grew for the work, I just kept taking the next step as it revealed itself. I was open to opportunities that came my way. Other times, I made the opportunities happen. I believed with every fiber of my being that I had a purpose, that it would become clear to me. I was always all in, creating an artistic, fulfilling, vibrant life; that's my personality too.

Now I looked around me and was filled with gratitude and a certain kind of amazement at all the magic we had conjured in such a short time. I operated a strong and growing business that comprised the salon in Beverly Hills, a corporate office, a warehouse, manufacturing partners, and a team of ABH-trained estheticians serving Nordstrom customers, as well as a presence in other retailers like Sephora, Ulta Beauty, and more.

I had worked hard for the past decade to connect with our customers. We kept up a massive effort with media interviews, in-store demonstrations, and new product output. Fortunately, I had a lot of natural energy. That voice from my childhood was always in my head driving me forward: *Work hard, don't complain, figure it out.* I viewed the world in a certain magnetic way, with curiosity and positivity, and I was fortunate to be able to share that energy with others, getting them excited too. I still traveled cross-country to Nordstrom stores almost every weekend for special events and to work hands-on with customers. I made it a priority to attend industry events, seminars, and beauty summits as I believe it is so important for entrepreneurs and leaders to go to gatherings like these to keep up with trends and meet people. It is one success secret I always share. These interactions helped build invaluable relationships within the industry. We developed a pro palette of eyebrow powder for makeup artists. It had eleven colors for use with their professional kit, whereas general consumers would purchase only the one color that suited them. I loved talking with these fellow artists. Their expertise and technical feedback were invaluable to making my products better and better.

I had help, of course, with all the outreach and consumer education. My niece Luca, among other people, joined our traveling team. In addition to managing the salon, she took on larger financial and operational roles within the company. I could see her head spinning the first time she came with us to Cosmoprof North America at the Las Vegas Convention Center. We had flown in early that morning and went right to the convention floor, even though we were hot and a little bit sleepy. Our booth was literally mobbed! It was the busiest booth in the whole convention center, and the only one that had scores of people lined up. That same day, I gave a seminar in the auditorium. Every seat was taken and a nearby room was provided for the overflow to watch on a huge TV screen. I asked the team to chat with people as they waited for the doors to open. When one woman found out Luca worked with me, she quite literally let out the type of loud scream usually reserved for rock stars or celebrities. It was an amazing moment. It felt like a great big hug of acknowledgment, and it was clear the impact we were making. But now was not the time to be complacent.

We were working harder than ever, but I was beginning to wonder if we could be working *better*? The pace, while wildly exciting, was not sustainable for the long term.

## Being Instagrammable

When Claudia came to me with her idea, I was ready to explore Instagram. I trusted Claudia's instincts: She knew our company from the ground up. She knew our customers, the marketplace, and the technology. Being open to new ideas, in my opinion, is what transforms good businesses into great ones. Being the first to market with an idea, product, or service was an old-school rule for business success. I suspected that being among the early adopters in a new medium could have the same impact. From the beginning, I had been passionate about teaching our customers to select the right product and apply it to their own unique features. This seemed like an opportunity to do that in a new medium. And we were reaching capacity in the way we were working, traveling every weekend to a different city to connect with customers. Claudia's idea came at the right time. We had everything to gain and nothing to lose at this point, and so, as they say, we put our pinky toe into the pool to test the water.

Claudia supervised the design, initial photos, and personally posted the pictures. We watched and waited together for the molecules and atoms we sent into the cosmos to gather shape and take form. And then, the response happened. We were soon getting thousands of likes. It was exhilarating! Our lives changed in a moment. We became obsessed with this new way of "talking" to our customers. The first thing I did before I got out of bed every morning was to reach for my phone and open Instagram. I was on it all day until I went to bed at night. Claudia and I responded to every comment ourselves. Every day there was more and more. The fast pace of our lives got faster, the internet being a universe that never sleeps.

It hit me just how many more people we were now reaching. When we traveled to Nordstrom locations or conferences and spent time speaking with clients about the products, we would reach maybe one hundred people a day, more at a seminar. It was all we could do with the time constraints. But when we posted those images, we had instant communication with our customers worldwide. We were having one-on-one conversations and building authentic relationships with our customers and beauty enthusiasts, just as we did in the salon or at Nordstrom, but at any time of day, and the customers were from everywhere. A woman commented that she wished she had our Brow Wiz product where she was. I asked, "What's your address? I'll send you one." It turned out that she was in India!

We had a fan all the way in India. It was then that I realized the kind of massive reach social media was going to give us. I had grown up in a Communist country isolated from other nations, from progress. Any communication with the rest of the world was done in secret, in little glimmers. Now we could openly communicate with people who lived in even the most remote regions. I was able to directly message women from India, Europe, and even Communist countries, which was personally gratifying to me. As the messages mounted from everywhere, telling us about the beauty, joy, and playfulness we were adding to people's lives, I felt even more committed to embracing new technologies that crossed borders and opened the world. I felt I was truly in my purpose, experiencing the destiny that had been whispering to me since I was a girl.

Our followers were passionate about makeup, we knew. We wanted to know everything about them: what they liked; what they wanted; what was their perfect, ideal product that was missing on the market. Everything we created based on those conversations, we shared with them, and we gave credit to our followers. Our tutorials, techniques, and products were not only being seen and utilized by people around the world, but also by the growing number of makeup artists and experts in the beauty space. They would soon be dubbed beauty influencers and content creators, those whose first pictures and posts were from makeshift studios in the corners of basements, bedrooms, or bathrooms.

As a person who came to this country with nothing, I knew the value of a helping hand was priceless. The beauty community had embraced me as one of their own from the start. I knew that when I was in the position to do so, I wanted to give back. I always believed it was important to lift others up, even those who might be competitors. What you give is what you receive in return. There is enough room in the business for everyone. I am proud to have been at the start and contributed to the growth of an entirely new field. We mentored a whole generation of influencers and content creators on Instagram, many of whom went on to build their own businesses. These inspiring pioneers in turn have not only contributed to the beauty industry through their tutorials and social media presence on Instagram and other platforms but have also paved the way for other creatives. Their artistry and vision made them trusted voices who continue to inspire and shape the landscape of beauty and lifestyle content online. I want to acknowledge the contributions of these OG influencers, including Amrezy, Chrisspy, Mac Daddy, Manny MUA, Christen Dominique, Jaclyn Hill, Desi Perkins, Jeffree Star, Patrick Starrr, Shayla, Tamanna, Tati Westbrook, and, later on, James Charles, NikkieTutorials, and many others.

Collaborating with such talented individuals was not only creative for Claudia and me but also built a sense of community within the beauty industry. My circle expanded tenfold as I opened my arms, my experience, and my own network to these young artists. We held gatherings at my house. Over afternoon tea or homemade dinners at my dining table, with the scent of brightly colored flower arrangements to inspire us, or evening drinks poolside, we would share stories, insights, and challenges that we mutually faced in working the art space of this new medium.

While all of us worked in high-touch visual fields—makeup, hairstyling, skincare—it took new skills to translate this expertise to an audience through the cold medium of a camera eye. Lighting and sound were new factors to consider, but not unfamiliar to us in the Hollywood movie business environment.

I keenly remembered what it was like being on a shoestring budget, counting every penny. So we found a way to contribute equipment—ring lights, microphones—so these influencers and creators could better connect with their audiences.

We always sent PR packages to them. As the platform began to grow and buzz around it started to build, we organically included Instagram as a part of our new product launch marketing, involving influencers in big makeup events and seasonal or themed campaigns. Later, we also developed affiliate programs where content creators could earn commissions for products sold through their referral links. Now, of course, digital and social media campaigns have become part of every brand's marketing. But with Claudia's vision, we were there right at the beginning, authentically a part of this new digital revolution. It would be years before other major brands entered the space. At this time, it was a more intimate, more informal environment. Instagram was just a community of creative people sharing their enthusiasm for makeup. Everything that became standard later was being done for the first time. The rules of etiquette and engagement were just

> **Social media did two incredible things for Anastasia Beverly Hills . . . it gave us a platform to showcase our products to a young, new audience . . . and it allowed us to celebrate and bring visibility to incredible talent.**
>
> —Claudia "Norvina" Soare

being established. We were fueled by the excitement of experimentation and imagination. Anastasia Beverly Hills became associated with innovation. We were just getting started.

## Business Comes Down to Dollars and Sense

We always had our ears open to what was happening in the industry. There was growing conversation about reinventing eye shadow palettes. The idea of a palette itself was not new. Elizabeth Arden had created the first "Arden Eye Shadow" in 1919, coining the term *eye shadow*. Later, eye shadows and palettes were also popularized by Hollywood studio artists Max Factor and Helena Rubinstein. Through the 1960s, '70s, and '80s, brands like Yardley London, Maybelline, CoverGirl, and Clinique offered their versions. In 1998, Urban Decay offered its first brightly colored eye shadow palette. In 2001, MAC Cosmetics offered a limited edition seasonal palette. In 2010, Urban Decay's Naked Palette, which was embraced by the beauty industry, showcased a neutral look.

Now something bold was bubbling up in the culture. Claudia was ready for it with high-quality luxurious formulas and exquisite colors. Anastasia Beverly Hills brow designs, cleanly shaped and brushed up, were trending. On the runways and in real life, fashion and makeup colors were bold, bright neon. In 2014, Claudia came to me with another pioneering idea. She wanted to partner with Instagram makeup artists to create products together, combining our talents and audiences.

I could feel Claudia's enthusiasm, and to be frank, I was excited about the idea too. We had taken our time behind the scenes to develop our cosmetics line, sorting through and perfecting all the complexities, regulations, and forms of distribution that went into expanding our line from brows to the makeup category. Now, with so much momentum behind us, it seemed like the right time to launch something new and bespoke. I knew that there was a brief window of time, a moon sliver of an opening when innovation and technology first intersect, in which a business needs to act or lose to a nimbler competitor.

I had also learned to do our due diligence before taking a business risk. This meant to consider every angle with a dispassionate mindset. Claudia and I got into it together. Were we able to handle the increased production, if needed? Did this align with our image as a brand? Was this the right next move? Did we have the financial capability to underwrite this endeavor to our high standards? Claudia and I called an "all-hands-on-deck" meeting with our department heads. Whatever we decided to do, we would need to gear up and do it quickly.

I believe in making the bet and taking the risk; that's how I came to America, that's how I opened the salon, that's how I partnered with Nordstrom, Sephora, Ulta Beauty, and others. It is part of the magic formula for building a big, beautiful life. There is no guarantee of success. It always takes a leap of hope, wonder, and faith. I believe in dreaming bold dreams in business, but also in keeping my feet grounded in finances that supported the people who worked with me—and their families. Creatives, artists, dreamers often don't want to talk about money. Entrepreneurs and leaders can't afford to ignore this truth: Money is the engine of business. Money is the resource that makes the start-up, expansion, gallery, salon, or digital platform possible. Managing cash flow, which is the circular flow of income, investment, and expenses, is an art, a dance, and an imperative. It is the heartbeat of a healthy business. I felt that I needed to keep my finger on the pulse. Luca and I, along with a comptroller and our accounting team, managed all the finances ourselves. Luca has been an essential part of our business journey. For so many years, she stood by my side, helping me make countless decisions. From the beginning, I recognized her immense potential, and she has certainly lived up to every expectation I had.

Now, after twenty years together, Luca is an integral part of the company. Her journey has been nothing short of inspiring, and I couldn't be prouder of all that she has accomplished. She is organized, meticulous, and strives for correctness in everything she does. We were always mindful of how we spent each dollar, knowing it would reflect on our EBITDA (earnings before interest, taxes, depreciation, and amortization). For anyone who wants to start or is running a business, I want to express how important it is to have a healthy EBITDA. It is an indicator of a company's operational efficiency, focusing on earnings generated from core business activities and excluding factors that can obscure profitability, such as financing and accounting decisions. A strong EBITDA indicates healthy cash flow, the cash-generating ability to do business, which is vital for a company to invest in growth. It is essential for demonstrating a company's profitability, attracting investment, and supporting strategic initiatives.

Thanks to the diligence and attention to detail of our team, we were able to achieve some of the best margins in the beauty industry, a fact we only discovered later. In 2018, our company was evaluated at $3 billion. I am incredibly grateful for everyone's support and commitment. We did not hire a CFO until 2019.

As an entrepreneur, and now the steward of a company that employed a few hundred people, I took the cost-benefit analysis of any business risk very seriously. It was no longer the early days when I was alone in my room at Juan Juan. I was keenly aware that it wasn't just my own livelihood at stake.

I leaned into the method that I have used to guide my business growth since I first opened the salon: Only invest as much as you can afford to lose, while holding cash in reserve as a safety net. It is a principle that I have found to be rock-solid, whether you are running a small business out of one room or a global enterprise. Having a hands-on familiarity with our finances has always been invaluable to me in deciding to take risks with a sense of calculated confidence. I think that experience, instinct, intuition, and timing also played a role. There is something else too: a kismet, a moment where hard work, luck, and destiny align.

## Taking a Chance on Yourself

When standing at a crossroads or evaluating an opportunity, I rely on my Rule #4: *Always Take a Chance on Yourself.* I never want fear of making a mistake or overanalyzing to immobilize my company or hold me back from doing the best I can. If you don't try, you never know what you could have accomplished. Sometimes you just have to dive into the deep end of the pool and trust the process, even if you're not fully sure about the outcome. As a leader, this leap will test your courage and your resilience.

> You can't be that kid standing at the top of the waterslide, overthinking it. You have to go down the chute.
>
> —Tina Fey, actress, comedian, author

We crunched the numbers, analyzed our cash flow, and came to the dollar amount we could afford to allocate while still being able to expand our product line into makeup in a stylish and artistic way that represented our sensibility. Then I stopped to breathe and listen to the voice inside. The alignment of the stars in that particular year had been so bountiful as we embraced the zeitgeist. I knew we had to do this. Side-by-side with my daughter, I said yes, and it was one of the best decisions I ever made. Anastasia Beverly Hills moved into a new era.

Even though we had a bump in the road with the body care line, this time manufacturing technology had caught up to our creative vision, giving us the ability to offer our customers something truly bold and innovative. Claudia's groundwork and artistry opened the path for us to expand into our trendsetting makeup line.

We went back to our manufacturers, many located in the US and Italy, for the best ingredients, chemists, and technologies, creating the best color stories. Science, art, design, and balance, the golden ratio underpinned everything we did. We worked hard on every detail of the tools and kits, every formula, every shade. We developed the products with an extreme purpose in mind. We wanted our customers to be able to get pro-level results without being a pro. We designed our makeup products so they could be used by a master makeup artist as well as by a beginner. The ingredients used to create the colors in cosmetics were sourced from around the world and brought to our manufacturers in Italy. Different batches coming from different countries and environments can slightly change the final color. This is a challenge to any manufacturer, but we would not accept anything less than top-notch. When customers reach for one of our products, I want them to feel they can count on the same results every time—a taupe will always be the same taupe. Even to this day, I personally approve every new order of brow products, and for good reason. While the manufacturers maintain the same formula, the raw materials are sometimes sourced from different companies. This means that, for example, a red powder pigment can vary slightly either with a cooler or warmer undertone. This can affect the final color, making it distinct from our standard shade.

This process can be challenging, as the initial appearance may seem similar to the standard color. Therefore, I must maintain close communication with the manufacturer to adjust the percentages of color or ingredients as needed. Although the approval process is lengthy, it is essential to ensure that we deliver the highest quality and consistency in our products. Claudia oversees the makeup line in the same way.

It goes back to what I learned in my mother's shop and reinforced through my own experience with our retail partners: Customer experience is everything. I will never forget that Anastasia Beverly Hills was built with the support of thousands of individual people around the world. We work for them. Every day, I want them to have the best products and service that we can deliver. Now, with all this in place, we were ready to reach out to potential partners.

## Excellence Is Always the Key to Success

It was a very exciting time for our business. We were caught up in the momentum. Claudia was inspired by the artistry of the influencers she interacted with daily. She came up with the idea to create limited edition collaborations with some of these artists. It

215

would be something that fans could embrace online and in store and would bring Anastasia Beverly Hills artistry and innovations to new audiences.

The first makeup artist we approached was Amra Olević Reyes, known as Amrezy, who had garnered a large fan base on Instagram and YouTube. Amrezy was known for her style and flawless makeup looks. Claudia and Amrezy had similar aesthetics, and our first collaboration was born. In 2014, we launched our limited edition Amrezy Palette. It was audacious, stunning. The shadows were buttery soft yet had intense color payoff. We sold it exclusively on our website first and then with other retailers. It was a phenomenal success both in sales and in buzz—two important metrics in the beauty category.

That same year we also collaborated with makeup artist Tamanna Roashan, known as @DressYourFace on Instagram, to release the Tamanna Palette. This eye shadow palette was designed for the 2014 holiday season and featured ten shades suitable for creating various looks. It also included five "Get the Look" cards with step-by-step tutorials by Tamanna herself. In summer 2014 we collaborated with Maja Janeska, who used the name Maya Mia and the handle @Maya_Mia_Y on Instagram, on the Maya Mia Eye Shadow Palette. We followed with our own iconic Anastasia Beverly Hills bestselling palettes: Modern Renaissance, Soft Glam, Sultry, and Contour Kit, as well as others like Subculture and Prism that garnered avid fans.

Claudia launched her own line of artistry palettes, *Norvina*, with the volume one palette offering options for customers who loved and wanted more colors and intensity. Our production amped up—from contour and lip palettes to a full line of cosmetics, including brow products, foundations, eye shadows, and more.

*Fashionista* called us the buzziest brand on the internet. Claudia's digital marketing innovations were being recognized in the wider beauty world. In 2016, Claudia was named on *Women's Wear Daily*'s "10 Most Wanted List: The 10 Most In-Demand Execs in Digital Fashion and E-Commerce."

We went on to work with some of the best and brightest in the beauty industry. Each collaboration was a special experience with an extraordinary artist. I couldn't be prouder of each of these creative, innovative, hardworking visionaries. I celebrate their success. I always say I am not here to build entrepreneurs; I am here to build *icons*. In all these cases, they most certainly are icons. Over the next few years, we collaborated with:

- **Mario Dedivanovic (Makeup by Mario):** Master Palette by Mario (2016) offered a versatile range of colors that appealed to professionals and beauty enthusiasts.

- **Nicole Guerriero:** Nicole Guerriero Glow Kit (2017) combined high-quality formulas and shades that enhanced a variety of skin tones. Known for her vibrant personality, exceptional makeup skills, and her ability to connect with her audience through authentic content.

- **Jackie Aina:** Jackie Aina EyeShadow Palette (2019) showcased her commitment to inclusivity, featuring colors that cater to deeper skin tones. Jackie uses her platform not only to share her artistry but also to educate and inspire change, making her a powerful voice in the influencer space.

- **Alyssa Edwards:** Alyssa Edwards EyeShadow Palette (2019) captured her bold aesthetic. Known for her vibrant personality and drag artistry, Alyssa brings a unique flair to the beauty community making entertaining and instructive beauty tutorials.

- **Carli Bybel:** Carli Bybel EyeShadow Palette (2019) highlighted her artistic vision, featuring shades that are both wearable and versatile. Carli's relatable blend of beauty, fashion, and lifestyle content has attracted an engaged and diverse audience.

- *RuPaul's Drag Race*, a show that Claudia and I have long admired. From the very beginning, we were captivated by the incredible talent of the artists. Their ability to transform strong features into soft, delicate looks showcases a profound understanding of facial proportions. Through the art of makeup, they skillfully minimize certain features with contouring while enhancing others using highlights. To support these talented contestants, we developed contour cream kits specifically for the show, designed to help them achieve the perfect depth and dimension in their looks. Each artist demonstrates remarkable skill, using makeup to create the balance and proportions they desire.

- *America's Next Top Model*, which featured our products for the contestants' makeup looks, bringing us deeper into the fashion world.

Claudia's bold leadership and artistic vision in collaborating with these influencers presented Anastasia Beverly Hills with exciting opportunities that exponentially expanded our visibility and business. Our venture into makeup had far exceeded our original projections and expectations. Now I had the confidence, based on real results, to make further investments in both the digital space and in extending our product line. With Instagram excitement and collaborations fueling us, Anastasia Beverly Hills transformed from the place for brows to where people could find all aspects of beauty to look and feel like their best selves. Demand for our products around the world was now outpacing distribution. Our retail partners wanted to expand our footprint in stores and internationally. New retailers were knocking at our doors to carry our line.

I was now CEO, and Claudia the president, of an expanding international operation that saw the name Anastasia Beverly Hills on displays and counters around the globe, with all the risks and all the potential growth that could bring. All that had happened in such a short period of time filled me with wonder and gratitude. I couldn't help but reflect back to the time I spent in the library in Sherman Oaks long ago, and the spark that had ignited this journey—the leap of imagination, the kismet, the aha moment to connect the golden ratio formula with brows. I was still fired up, still wanting to do more for my customers, and still charging forward to new heights and a new era for our company.

# The Risk/Reward Primer

Every opportunity in business and life brings with it risks as well as rewards. If you don't try, you never know what you could accomplish. Move forward with calculated confidence. Use these tools to bet on yourself without breaking the bank, whether you're starting a podcast or hoping to launch a company.

### Crunch the Numbers
Gather all the numbers associated with whatever it is you're weighing up. Look thoroughly at everything. Keep your eye on cash flow. Make sure that there is the infrastructure in place to deliver products and services for the short term and long term if the venture takes off.

### The Crystal Ball
Envision the upside, whether that's brand visibility, reputation, buzz, investment, or return.

### Do Your Research
Innovation is offering something new or reimagining a novel way to build an existing product or service. Look for a gap in the marketplace. Figure out your offering's unique value proposition.

### Listen to Other People's Ideas
No one can think of everything themselves; collaboration is key for success. Ask trusted family, friends, or colleagues for their opinion.

### Don't Be Afraid to Play Big
Unleash your greatness. Without risk there is no reward.

CHAPTER TWELVE

# Lead Like Your Business Depends on It

To create something exceptional, your mindset
must be relentlessly focused on the smallest detail.

—GIORGIO ARMANI

The dream I had to touch women's lives everywhere through beauty, which seemed so incredibly audacious when I launched my first brow kit, was now coming true beyond my wildest hopes and expectations. We were becoming a global company. Instagram had opened instant communication with enthusiasts around the world who wanted our products. Sephora built locations where the world could come to experience Anastasia Beverly Hills in real life. Our business was continuing to expand in Ulta Beauty and at other retailers. It felt like we were touching the stars. I knew that my feet needed to stand firmly on the ground while my eyes were fixed on the horizon of all that was still to come. We couldn't let up now.

There is a secret I learned over the years about growing a business and remaining successful that I share with entrepreneurs, leaders, and managers who ask me. In business and in life, every day is a reset. Sure, we can celebrate our accomplishments, and I do. But the truth is that even the most successful business needs to continuously work to capture the imagination of its customers and stay ahead of the competition every day. The minute you stop innovating, someone else comes along right behind you with something new. Even though I was the head of a global company, I still leaned into my Rule #5: *Lead Like Your Business Depends on It. Because It Does.*

Everything in the universe has an energy, and a company or organization does as well. The urgency, the excitement, the vision, the positivity and magic start at the top and extend to all the details that make a difference to customers. I think a leader needs to have a vision, a strategy of what the company is going to do, but at the same time understand every aspect of their business and be unafraid to roll up their sleeves and be where the work of the company happens. How exactly do we spend the money? I still sign the checks and read all the invoices. No batch of makeup products goes into production without me testing them. I lead by example and by staying involved. I believe that excellence is in the details.

## Every Day Is an Opportunity to Do Better

When I had made the decision to pivot and embrace the self-serve retail environments of Sephora and Ulta Beauty. I faced a philosophical as well as business challenge. My approach to beauty had grown out of my salon beginnings, where I taught clients how to choose and apply products, worked with my own staff, and then later trained the estheticians at Nordstrom in the ABH Golden Ratio Shaping Technique. Now I wondered how I would be able to share my methods and build strong relationships with my customers without actually having a trained technician on site.

While it is not traditionally the job of the CEO, I was involved with Claudia and my team in designing our "gondolas," or displays, to make sure that they explained the products to the customers clearly so they would know how to use them. We wanted to create a sleek, glamorous, elevated look that highlighted and depicted the artistry authentic to our brand and also showcased our products in a realistic fashion. As the Sephora and Ulta Beauty model was all about how the customer got to play with the makeup, I knew that even the smallest detail could be the one thing that might disappoint or delight a customer and make or break a sale. We had to think about how to offer customers a clear and organized way to explore the wide range of Anastasia Beverly Hills offerings while still making it easy for them to match correct colors.

As our reputation and product line grew exponentially, so did the size of the displays. Between 2017 and 2019, Ulta Beauty expanded our space from three feet (brow only stores) to full nine-foot gondolas in over five hundred stores. We grew as Ulta Beauty did. Today, we are in all their stores.

We didn't take these expansions lightly. The bigger the business, the more costly the mistakes are—both financially and to customer loyalty. While Claudia and I are both very artistry minded, we looked at the construction with different but complementary points of view. Claudia's leading thought was the aesthetics, the colors, and the crowd appeal. She would think, *What story is this display telling?* I was very focused on the practical aspects of what the display did or didn't do for the customer or retailer. I would put myself into my customer's shoes, as I have always done, and think, *How easily can I get my hand into the unit to pick up the product or identify the shade I want?* Or from the retailer perspective: *How many additional pieces of back stock could be stored in the gondola (display) to make sure it is not sitting empty if someone comes up and says, "I want a Brow Wiz in Ebony, where is it?"* I worked with our design team to house all the products we could humanly fit into the display so that if a customer reached for them, they were there. My five years training in technical design that I learned in school came in handy, even if I thought at the time that I would never use it. So learn everything you can when you are young, you never know when you will apply it.

While I was contemplating this dramatic shift to staff-less in-store retail, I realized that I no longer had to figure out everything myself as I once had to do in the beginning. I had support now.

I met with every department—finance, marketing, social media, and product development—to get their input. We brainstormed and whiteboarded. The solutions we came up with were a combination of new and time-tested approaches—we shared digital tutorials with application techniques on Instagram, our website, and elsewhere on socials; we included instructions on the product or its package; and I participated in many national TV interviews with demonstrations on shows like the *Today* show and *Good Morning America* where I gave how-to information to millions of viewers.

We never put out a product that we were not completely in love with ourselves. And every time we had a new launch, the entire education team worked on pro tips and video tutorials to make sure our clients got the best use out of their new product. We imagined our consumer as the ABH "prosumer"—someone who expects and deserves professional-level products, even if they're not in the beauty profession. We designed our products with them in mind.

I also went on the road again, just like I had with Nordstrom. I traveled to all the new Sephora locations to do personal appearances, meet customers, and dedicate myself to teaching the Sephora cast members (makeup artists and salespeople) who would be on-site managing the displays and answering customer questions as needed. I still to this day do seminars, video tea parties, and other internal events with Sephora staff around the world. As Sephora opened new locations in the US, Europe, India, the Middle East, Australia, Asia, Mexico, and South America (including Brazil), we expanded with them. I once even pushed through the rowdy crowds at the annual Rio Carnival to go to a store event, despite the safety concerns of my protective attorney and friend Jeff Smith. It is such an honor to be so in-demand, and to arrive in a location to jam-packed events with queues forming outside the door. I refused to miss an opportunity to connect with customers who had RSVP'd for the standing-room-only event and were waiting for me. I always made it a practice to stay to the end of any event to talk with the cast members. I think they deserve the love because they show so much support for our brand, and I wanted to let them know how much I appreciated them. Young managers often said to me, "How can you stand for so many hours in your high heels?"

When I work with customers, the excitement keeps me from being tired or feeling any aches or pains. Instead, I feel exhilarated. When I am in this zone, I can keep going nonstop. I have always been this way. I have a lot of natural energy and enthusiasm. These are qualities many leaders have. I can draw upon them to work long hours at the salon all day, review finances into the night with Luca, and make business decisions while still giving my clients and my staff my attention. People might call this multitasking, but I think of it more as the ability to micro-focus. I stay in the present. I give each moment my all and then move on.

I feel the same focus and dedication during all of my personal appearances. Making women feel beautiful through my techniques gives me so much joy; it is electric. It fills me with energy. I always stayed until the very end of an event, even when only staff remained. It was important to take the time to talk with everyone. I care about building "hero products," which are beloved by our customers, and about always delivering our best. How else could I truly learn about problems, trends, or what customers needed now?

In addition to Nordstrom and Sephora, I also made personal appearances at Ulta Beauty locations around the country. I met Ulta Beauty's chief merchandizing officer, a strikingly elegant woman with large expressive eyes named Monica Arnaudo, when she was at Nordstrom. She became a longtime friend. I was honored when she invited us to meet with Ulta Beauty's own staff at their headquarters in Bolingbrook, Illinois. Their team transformed their biggest conference room into a memorable "Anastasia Event" and celebration. I did the brows of everyone who attended. It was an incredible opportunity to get to know all the people working to support my brand as well as do some training too. Under the direction of Kecia Steelman, president and CEO, we continue to have a strong and productive partnership, growing our companies and employees together. She is an exceptional and talented leader who has made remarkable strides in the beauty industry.

Everything I learned on the road I would bring back and pour into our development, infrastructure, people, and company. I realized long ago that no one person can think of everything themselves; innovation comes from conversation. Claudia has that same sensibility. Our products always solve customer problems because we've listened and learned from customers, partners, and our team. We stick to quality and education. I think having this hands-on approach, while still being able to scale our business, has helped our company stay true to our customer-centric roots. It's why our brand resonates with so many people.

## To Build Something Exceptional, You Need Exceptional People

I believe there are two pillars that are the foundations of any business, but my business in particular: products and people. There are the products that make customers look and feel their best. And there are the people my company serves, both my customers and my employees. I see my employees as an extension of myself, as extended family. They are more important than anything else, because without them my business can't grow or thrive. I have many people in my company who have been with me for ten or even twenty-plus years who refer to themselves as "ABH lifers." Like Mary-Catherine Mellon, our executive director of global brand marketing, who we call Mcat. Another ABH lifer is Tom Colley, VP of e-commerce. I get a lot of joy from the fact that people build entire careers at Anastasia Beverly Hills; I feel that it is the ultimate compliment as a leader.

As an entrepreneur and boss, I've learned that how I approach changing circumstances and mistakes—as well as triumphs—makes a dramatic impact on my employees, both their emotions and performance. What I can do to help my employees and business thrive is to lift, inspire, motivate, and believe in them. Like every form of energy in the natural world, positivity is circular. *Your passion and compassion, your personal integrity, and your presence can be inspirational.* When I wake up each morning, I consciously put myself into a positive frame of mind, ready to tackle any challenges head-on. Once you embrace this mindset, everything that comes at you during the day is filtered through the lens of possibility, mindful intent, and even humor. Let's not forget that life is funny sometimes, and beauty is a fun thing to do! I believe we need to be serious when it comes to serious things, but there should inherently be fun to the daily grind, as it were. I'm the first one in a meeting to laugh or crack a joke.

It has been my experience that productivity and profit go up when team members sincerely feel respected and valued and enjoy what they do. At the end of the day, leadership comes down to being consistent, persistent, and thoughtful in building the culture you want to create in your business and setting the intention for success.

I want my company to produce exceptional results for our customers, vendors, and partners, so I hire the most exceptional people to lead every department. And I listen to them. When faced with a business challenge or new goal, I don't want to just make a decision on my own, top-down. I talk with my whole team and hear everyone's opinion, because everybody has a different point of view that may be helpful or important to factor into my thought process. Maybe they could come up with a solution or a faster, better, more efficient process than I could. And they often did. While I might make the ultimate decision, they were better decisions as a result of everyone's input.

A CEO can also learn so much about their own business by talking to everybody in production and the warehouse. It is important to stay connected with the process of *making* and *doing*. I love walking the warehouse distribution center. It is always a noisy whirl of activity. It is amazing to me that I have such dedicated people making sure that the products are in perfect condition, properly packaged, and promptly shipped to our vendors and individual customers. My warehouse facility is so large it reminds me of an airplane hangar.

I always talk with everyone. The truth is that not everything is perfect all the time. I believe that a good leader needs to make people feel safe to speak up when they feel like something is not working, so they can take action and solve the problem. I encouraged all my employees to share their issues and their ideas with me, whether in these casual conversations or in department meetings. I wanted people to feel empowered in their jobs, and to know that we would do anything to help them do their work better, faster, easier. Together we can solve any challenge. These walks through the warehouse kept me connected and confirmed to me something that I already knew: I had great people working for me up and down my organization.

I believe that the loyalty you get from your employees is the loyalty you give in return. COVID created unprecedented challenges to our business, like all others, and many of my employees felt the effects of these circumstances. As a leader, I made sure that I stayed visible and accessible to all my staff to create a sense of stability in such an uncertain time. We hoped to ride it out as best we could. Like other companies, we quickly transferred most of our employees from the physical office to virtual, and Zoom meetings filled my day. I helped employees in as many ways as possible, paying out of my own pocket to keep people going during this crisis time. I never forgot what I had felt during my hardest days in Romania and earliest days in America, and the miracle that even the smallest amount of care and generosity from another human being can bring.

During this time, we lost my longtime warehouse manager and old friend, Tino Stan, who had been with me from the beginning. He had been so important to me and was by my side for so many years. I am grateful for the contributions that he and so many other people made to my company.

COVID really put into focus something I already believed, that a leader's job extends to the larger world as well as the confines of a company. Building strong connections in your industry is critical, in both good times and downturns. We all need each other to thrive. I find it fulfilling to support other women, artists, dreamers, entrepreneurs—whether it is through personal or company financial donations, or sharing other resources like my time, advice, and support or promotion of their businesses and ventures. Giving back to people is of utmost importance to me in both business and life.

I would never forget the extended beauty community. I lent my leadership expertise to many makeup artists and new beauty founders during this hard time through scholarship programs and partnerships such as the Blue Heron Foundation and others doing important work, such as Baby2Baby and Susan G. Komen. I also supported young entrepreneurs including Tamanna Roashan, makeup artist and founder of DYF Beauty; Diana Madison, founder of Diana Madison Beauty; Rahama Wright, founder of Shea

Yeleen, a social impact beauty company; and Alisa Tovmanyan and Eliza Glants of J'Adore Les Fleurs, masters of the craft of flower arrangements and my go-to florist for events.

These exceptional dreamers have remained in my circle of female entrepreneurs and friends to this day. It means so much to me to be able to support their bold ideas and put a spotlight on their accomplishments. I want every woman to be seen, to be heard, as I have been, and to know that her contribution is significant. Just as I hope I can inspire other women, I have been lucky to have had so many women inspire me and help me to grow. One such person is Nadia Comăneci Conner, a fellow Romanian immigrant, who holds a special spot in my heart. She was the first person in history to score a perfect ten in the Olympics, doing so in 1976, and ultimately won five gold medals and became an Olympic legend. She works with her husband, American Olympic gymnast Bart Conner, winner of two gold medals, to inspire gymnasts, athletes, and others to positive performance.

Nadia's own story of defecting from Communist Romania in 1989, where, as a prized athlete, her life had been harshly monitored and controlled by the government, to start over in America is an example of fortitude, bravery, and perseverance, as well as discipline and determination. She is a legend who continues to inspire. In 2026 she will celebrate fifty years of the perfect ten. We both marvel at how far we have come from where we began, and the better life each of us built. I truly believe that a woman can do whatever she puts her mind to doing.

# The Leadership Essentials Kit

Keeping a focus on the future is critical for leaders in any business, organization, or artistic endeavor. It takes resiliency and fierce determination to manifest your vision and to take it from an idea to a success and keep it there.

### Lead with Confidence
You set the vision and direction of the company, inspire those who work with you to embrace that vision, and help them find their own greatness in the process.

### Be Adaptable and Resilient
The ability to pivot, adjusting strategies when information or conditions change, is critical to keep your business strong. Be open to new ideas and new technologies. The world is constantly moving, so move with it.

### Hire the Best People for the Job
If you want to do something exceptional, you need exceptional people on your team. Their success is your success too.

### Move Forward Decisively
Quick decisions can make the difference in staying ahead of competition and trends. Gather the data, trust your intuition, and take action.

### Believe in the Future
Invite in your imagination and passion to envision future possibilities and opportunities. Instead of focusing on what is, believe in what could be.

# Shaping the Life You Want

**Your beliefs become your thoughts. Your thoughts
become your words. Your words become your actions.
Your actions become your habits. Your habits become
your values. Your values become your destiny.**

—Mahatma Gandhi

One day in 2019, I got a call about a Sephora event that truly
stopped me in my tracks.

"Hi, Anastasia," said an upbeat voice on the phone. It was
Andreea Altay, who had worked with me for many years. She had
talked with a Sephora sales manager.

"They are opening a store in Bucharest, Romania. They would
really love for you to headline the event and the opening party,"
she said with excitement.

I couldn't breathe. I had so many emotions. It had been exactly
thirty years since I'd left Romania. I had been back a few times
over the years to see family, but this was something very different.
The girl who had been kicked out of class for wearing red boots
under her drab uniform, who had been relentlessly and ruthlessly
interrogated by police, who had fled to America and braved a

new life there as an immigrant because of the harsh government, was now being invited back as an international business success and honored guest. I felt a rush of absolute sweetness sweep over me from head to toe like the warm golden rays of the California sunshine. I finally exhaled.

"Anastasia, are you there?" I had almost forgotten that I was on the phone.

"Yes, of course I'll go," I said.

Claudia, my mother, and Luca all understood my sense of triumph and my tears as I stood waiting for the plane at LAX in the same terminal where I had once arrived as an immigrant with a baby, no English, no job, and no money. Just fear and hope.

In Bucharest, a sleek black town car picked me up from my hotel for the afternoon event. The Sephora store was located in the Băneasa Shopping City, a place bustling with activity. It is interesting how cities change, develop, and build on top of the past. When I grew up in Romania, there were no department stores; most free enterprise had been all but halted by Nicolae Ceauşescu's government. I could never have dreamed of this sort of shopping experience. Andreea Altay and Dorothy Constantin, the two statuesque beauties who greeted me at the door, were too young to remember. I had begun working with Andreea and Dorothy fifteen years earlier. They had a vision to open an Anastasia Beverly Hills salon in Bucharest, Romania. They were not only young and beautiful but incredibly smart and hardworking. I truly believed that I could mentor them to become the next generation of our beauty business. Today they are integral members of our international team.

As I walked through the noisy, colorful space, I couldn't help but feel the shadow of those past days lurking behind the bright lights and touching me. We carry our past with us, as my friend Patrick had taught me, but we can choose to discard the bad or hurtful memories and invite in the goodness of new experiences. And I chose to embrace that and let myself bask in the joy of the moment and all that it meant to me.

The Sephora store was decked out with black balloons with white lettering in the Sephora style, which said Sephora Loves Anastasia. There was a huge crowd of people squeezed together from the stage to the exits and up the stairs to a balcony promenade, which was also packed. The air literally crackled with excitement, the sound of laughter, and the buzz of conversation. I would not make my Sephora debut in Romania in muted colors, as I was once forced to wear. I met the crowd in a canary-yellow thin pencil dress that came past my knees, accented by a tiny black belt at the waist and my tallest black gladiator heels. They had built a raised platform for me. As I walked up to take my place, the only other thing on it besides me was a Hollywood-style ring spotlight taller than I was that gave me the perfect backlighting.

"Hello, Romania!" I shouted to the crowd. There were cheers and a standing ovation that lasted and lasted. I was one of their own and I had done good.

After I spoke, Dorothy led me on a meet and greet through the throngs of people. There was one young girl who hovered at the edges, her dark brown eyes wide open and luminous. She wore simple country clothes that almost reminded me of my grandmother. I turned to shake her hand, and she wrapped her arms around me in a big hug.

"Anastasia, I traveled by bus for five hours from Vaslui just so I could see you and tell you this. Thank you, thank you, thank you from the bottom of my heart for inspiring all of us."

I hugged her back and as I let go, she walked away quickly into the crowd. I never got her name. It seemed that all she wanted was to meet me face-to-face to tell me directly from her heart about how I had lifted her up. But it was her light that lifted *me* up right then and there in the middle of the crowd.

# Beauty is not about having a perfect face. It's about having a beautiful mind, a beautiful heart, and a beautiful soul.

I've been so blessed to meet a lot of well-known people, celebrities, and CEOs, but that quick exchange touched me so deeply. I counted it as one of my life's Oscar moments. I knew the deprivations so many women faced around the world, and still do in Romania, and what it took for her to make that trip, as Vaslui is known to be one of the poorest cities. To know that my work made such a profound difference was confirmation that all that had happened in my life, and all that I had gone through, had been for a reason. Destiny, hard work, and a little stardust had conspired together to bring me to this moment. I felt elated, energized, and humbled.

# Maybe helping other people is the best-kept beauty secret of all.

I had risked crossing an ocean, starting over with nothing, and taking a gamble on myself. I had followed my heart, mastered my craft, worked extremely hard, and figured things out. My dream was to inspire women from the biggest cities to the smallest communities and everywhere in between to feel and look their best, and I had accomplished it. I had gone back to where I started. Now I was ready to go *home* to America and Anastasia Beverly Hills. I looked forward to my next chapter to see all the joys, challenges, and magic the future would bring. For the moment, I felt complete.

There is an idea that success is a destination, a fixed point in the distance that beckons you like the North Star in the night sky or the pinnacle of Mount Everest. Static. Immutable. It might be defined by attaining a specific title, a prestigious award, or a certain amount of dollars saved. Once you reach it, you're done. You can stop striving and start shopping. Nothing is further from the truth in my experience. To me, *success is not an end in itself, but always the beginning of what comes next.* And there is always something next. There is always a new opportunity for change and growth, to find magic in yourself and share it with someone else. Each of us can make a difference in the world around us. Tomorrow holds even more than today.

# Beauty Begins the Moment
# You Decide to Be Yourself

We experience many chapters in our lives as we walk the path from where we began to where we want to be. Some are difficult, some are happy, and many are unexpected. I have shared my story with you in this book in the hope that some part of my experience and the lessons I've learned spark something in you. We are born into certain circumstances, but they don't have to define who we are. The true beginning is when you allow your heart to dream uncensored: *You have a purpose, a destiny.* I believe that every person who wants to be an entrepreneur, a leader, an artist, a creator of any kind can find their own way if they stop and listen to the little voice within them calling them to imagine, to innovate, and to invent. It is activated when we *choose* to be ourselves, whether we shout that out to the world boldly in bright colors and makeup or allow who we are to quietly define our everyday decisions. It takes courage and determination to manifest the dreams in your heart into being. *Don't give up. You can figure it out.*

There will be challenges every step of the way, of course, and you will need to work hard at every stage. But every chapter in your life offers a new chance to master your craft, to innovate, be curious, and be authentically yourself in everything you do. Don't worry about things you can't do or compare yourself with someone else. Claudia had once asked me, as we sat together at the kitchen table after I cooked a Sunday dinner, "Is it OK that I don't like to cook?" *You don't have to be good at everything; just focus on what you love to do.* If you don't like to cook, don't.

It is all about striking the balance that works for you. That is truly the **golden ratio of life**. Remember that beauty is about balance and proportion—not perfection. Life is challenging, figuring it out is messy, but you are enough as you are. Focus on mastering your craft; everything else will follow. I read somewhere that "Luxury is laughter and friends; luxury is hugs and kisses; being loved by people; being respected; having your parents alive; luxury is what money can't buy." Money is not the end goal, but it can be the jet fuel to make your dreams a reality. I found that sharing my abundance with family, friends, and the larger community of women gave joy and meaning to my success.

## We are unstoppable when we support each other.

There is something very powerful that happens when women come together to share their stories. My network, my circle of support, has grown over the years since I first gathered clients, industry professionals, and friends for dinners and drinks. Even now as I move forward in my passion to empower women by hosting seminars or weekend events that bring together beauty editors, influencers, beauty brand founders, friends, and celebrities who lend their support, it is still about the same thing to me: women lifting each other up in business and in life. I am grateful for all that came before, the battles won, the knowledge gained, and the life I created. I want to pay it forward.

For me, in this next chapter of my life, I want to spend my time supporting the greatness within all women that is waiting to be unleashed. I want to help women in all walks of life to rise to their highest heights and empower entrepreneurs, artists, leaders, and dreamers such as yourselves to live your dreams as you imagine them. It is my purpose and passion. It fills me with energy and hope.

Ultimately, it's about community—the support and encouragement we offer one another as we pursue our visions. You can create your own community that nurtures your talent and that you can nurture in return. Even with limited resources, your vision can soar. You may have to seek it out in different, new, and virtual spaces. You may have to make the first move to introduce yourself to someone new. Take that chance. Open your heart, reach for what could be, and ask, "How can I help?"

## Gratitude and Grace

I believe that everyone can shape the life they want. As I said in the beginning of this book, I am the proof. I dreamed beyond my wildest dreams and achieved them. I know that you too can find what is meaningful for your life. Find the courage to turn your passion into action. I am not saying this is easy; nothing is. I had setbacks and missteps, as we all do and will. But magic happens when you move through your life with grit, grace, generosity, and gratitude. The effort and love that we put into our pursuits and relationships truly define our success.

I could have never imagined, when I first stepped off that plane in LA so long ago as a new immigrant who didn't speak English and then went on to brave the odds of opening a salon focused on *brows*, that twenty-five years later I would be hosting an anniversary party attended by world-famous celebrities, models, business leaders, and friends old and new, including Jessica Alba, Alessandra Ambrosio, Monica Arnaudo, Priyanka Chopra, Cindy Crawford, Meena Lakdawala-Flynn, Desiree Gruber, Debbi Hartley-Triesch, Lori Harvey, Kris Jenner, Kim Kardashian, Gayle King, Heidi Klum, Jennifer Lopez, Maria Menounos, Artemis Patrick, Gelila Assefa Puck, Sharon Stone, Ashley Tisdale, Sofía Vergara, and Oprah Winfrey.

And they wanted to celebrate with *me*. It was the moment of a lifetime, my ultimate Oscar moment, made even more meaningful because I was able to host it in my own home. I love entertaining and setting a beautiful table for family and friends. It is like creating my own movie scene. That night, the incredible Colin Cowie planned the party, and he and his team transformed my dining room into a joyful, sensory delight. My table was set with my best china and silverware, and candlelight reflected from the Baccarat crystal glasses. Down the middle, spanning its full twenty-four-foot length end to end, was an overflowing abundance of flowers in my colors of pink, beige, and gold, filling the air with fragrance.

I stood looking at the table in the quiet before the party, my arms around my daughter, Claudia. We both wore elegant fitted black dresses. She looked beautiful with her long hair a stunning white blonde. I was proud to share the night with her, proud of who she is and her accomplishments, and of the harmony we have together in our lives and work.

The doorbell rang. The guests were arriving. I could hear Oprah's deep laugh. As I turned away from the dining room to greet them in the hallway just beyond the doors, my mind flashed back to another time. I was digging in the dirt behind my house in Romania to hide the family silver, which was my grandmother's proudest possession, so it wouldn't be confiscated by the government police knocking at the door. My fingernails were breaking, I was sweating with fear even though the temperature was frigidly cold. In an instant, I was back to greet my guests. I was here, now, a living testament that through hard work, drive, and grit, you can survive. You can thrive. America truly is the land of opportunity, like no other country in the world. A place where an immigrant can start with nothing and go on to build a better life, like I did. That very same family silver was now on the table at my party.

Embrace every moment as an opportunity to shine. When you do, your own light uplifts everyone around you. Your uniqueness is your strength, and every challenge you face is a chance to grow. Remember, you have the power to create your own path and inspire others along the way. Keep believing in possibilities. If you dream it, you can be it.

## The Magic I See in You

What I learned along the way through the magical Hollywood community, my family, my circle of friends, my clients and customers, and my retail partners is a very simple truth. Everything in friendship, business, and life is all about love. The love you give others and the love that comes back to you. My journey has taken me beyond my wildest dreams, from immigrant to successful entrepreneur. I am grateful to every person who supported me and Anastasia Beverly Hills.

And to you, my readers. Thank you for being a part of this journey too. I want to take a moment to remind you of the incredible potential that lies within you. The world is a vast canvas, and you hold the brush. You are capable of painting a masterpiece! Embrace the unique qualities and skills that make you who you are. Your individuality is your greatest strength, and it is these very traits that will guide you toward your dreams. Trust your instincts—they are the stars that will help you navigate through the darkest nights. Success is found in pursuing what ignites your passion, staying true to your beliefs, and making a difference in the lives of those around you. The world is eager for your contribution, and I am confident you will make a lasting impact.

## You've got this.
## I believe in you.
## You're ready.

# The Magic of Hollywood

**A TRUE ARTIST IS NOT ONE WHO IS INSPIRED BUT ONE WHO INSPIRES OTHERS.**

—Salvador Dalí

In the enchanting realm of Hollywood, a symphony of talent and creativity comes together to weave the magic that captivates the world. Behind the glimmering stars lies a dedicated team of professionals whose collective efforts fuel the industry's vibrancy. With over three decades in the beauty industry, I have had the privilege of working alongside incredible individuals—actors, executives, managers, agents, PR specialists, and clients from around the world who have visited my salon in Beverly Hills. They are the heart of my passion and the reason I wake up each day, filled with joy, eager to help others feel beautiful and confident.

When I immigrated to America, I chose to live in Los Angeles for the same reasons that everybody from everywhere wants to come here: It is the place of stardust and dreams, where everyone comes to be the best of themselves and be surrounded by the best.

It is about living the American success story: realizing one's potential and striving for greatness. Embracing the belief that anyone, whether they are an immigrant or born here, can achieve success and prosperity through hard work, determination, and opportunity.

I am reminded of that every day in little ways as I go about my life, but sometimes it comes sharply into focus through a dazzling moment. I was invited to *The Daily Front Row*'s Fashion Los Angeles Awards in 2024, where the incredible singer Doja Cat and others—including me—were honored. Kris Jenner presented me with an award. It was a glamorous night with a red carpet and celebrities all dressed in their most fashion-forward styles. I thought I would have fun, but I didn't expect to feel moved or leave with my head buzzing with creative ideas. Doja Cat got onto the stage wearing a fabulous lingerie-inspired outfit that drew applause. She presented an award to her stylist. Instead of talking about her own many accomplishments, she spent her time thanking all of those who created her look—her stylist, hairdresser, and makeup artist. She acknowledged that she is part of a community of creatives, *each one a master of their craft*, which turns artistic vision into reality.

I realized that so many of the celebrities I have gotten to know also supported many people around them just like Doja did. They are so generous in building the careers of those whose artistry they admire. One is my friend and client Cardi B, the multitalented singer and songwriter known for her bold personality and unique style, who always gives credit to her hairstylist, Tokyo Stylez; her fashion stylist, Kollin Carter; and her makeup artist, Erika La' Pearl. Another is Jennifer Lopez, who has elevated numerous artists to global recognition simply because she appreciates their talent and invites them to collaborate. She is an artist and a visionary. She knows exactly what she wants. When it comes time to choose her dress for a particular award, she already has a concept in mind that she shares with her hairstylist, makeup artist, and stylist. Jennifer consistently supports the talented individuals who bring her look to life, showcasing her commitment to uplifting others in the industry.

Others are like that too. Kim Kardashian, Kylie Jenner, Zendaya, Hailey Bieber, and so many incredible celebrities, style icons, entrepreneurs, and artists I've had the pleasure of meeting and being friends with are so generous in supporting the other artists and doers around them. They actively help build the careers of those they admire.

And I want to take a moment to thank them and shine a spotlight on them—all the masterful stylists, makeup artists, and beauty experts who make Hollywood what it is. To name a few from the many I've known:

Pat McGrath, the Dame, whose clients include Naomi Campbell, Kim Kardashian, and runway supermodels for whom she has created the most iconic looks with her innovative techniques and vibrant colors. She is also known for her expertise in special effects makeup, which adds an additional layer of creativity to her repertoire. Pat collaborated with John Galliano, known for his avant-garde and theatrical designs, for many years, and McGrath's makeup artistry complements this vision.

Jo Baker, who is known for her innovative approach to makeup artistry, creating memorable looks on the red carpet and at events for clients such as Gal Gadot, Lucy Boynton, Olivia Wilde, Margot Robbie, and more. I met Jo when we worked together with

Sharon Stone, who has been a longtime client and inspiration to us both.

Sir John, who is known for creating radiant skin and looks that blend classic modern styles for his clients, including Beyoncé and Winnie Harlow.

Lisa Eldridge, whose many celebrity clients include Kate Winslet, Dua Lipa, Emma Stone, and Keira Knightley, known for creating her natural, dewy looks that stun on the red carpet.

Michael Anthony, who has built a reputation for his ability to create stunning looks that enhance natural beauty, working with Ariana Grande and numerous celebrities.

Hung Vanngo, who works with Selena Gomez and other celebrities, is known for his ability to enhance natural beauty with well-defined eye shadow and soft romantic lip colors, as well as bold and trendy styles.

Ash K Holm, known for her transformative work with Jennifer Lopez and Kim Kardashian, is particularly skilled in enhancing features with flawless skin finishes, dramatic eye makeup, and perfectly sculpted eyebrows.

Etienne Ortega, whose artistry resonates with the unique styles of Christina Aguilera and Kris Jenner, creates stunning looks that combine glamour with artistry.

Mary Phillips, whose clients include Jennifer Lopez, Kendall Jenner, Hailey Bieber, and many other high-profile people in entertainment, creates a fresh, polished aesthetic, often blending classic techniques with modern trends.

Ariel Tejada, whose precision and flair have made him a favorite among beauty enthusiasts and stars like Kylie Jenner. His artistic skills and creativity allow him to beautifully enhance features.

Rokael Lizama, whose adaptability has earned him recognition with luminaries such as Beyoncé. He is known for creating flawless skin, expertly blended eye shadow, and radiant highlights, which all enhance the natural beauty of his clients.

Mario Dedivanovic, who collaborated with Anastasia Beverly Hills on the Master Palette by Mario, is known for his flawless skin techniques and signature contouring for clients. Mario has created iconic looks that enhance natural beauty while delivering a glamorous finish.

Derrick Rutledge, who is a highly respected celebrity makeup artist and beauty expert who has built a reputation for his ability to create polished, timeless looks. I always enjoyed spending time with Derrick when we worked with Oprah.

Erika La' Pearl, recognized for her versatility and creativity, has contributed to numerous iconic looks in Hollywood, music, and fashion. We met and worked together with Cardi B on her brows and makeup.

Anthony Merante, a remarkable artist whose creativity and talent have significantly enriched our Anastasia Beverly Hills campaigns. His exceptional work with renowned figures like Taraji P. Henson, Iggy Azalea, Kimora Lee Simmons, and many others showcases his unparalleled artistry and versatility.

Carl Ray, known for his ability to create polished, clean, and elegant looks. We would see each other when we worked with former First Lady Michelle Obama.

This extraordinary community continues to push the boundaries of beauty, crafting looks that ignite trends and inspire millions of fans and other makeup artists with their work.

The work of hairstylists also plays a crucial role in shaping the overall look of celebrities, especially on the red carpet. Notable hairstylists include:

Jen Atkin, who is celebrated for her influential presence in the beauty industry and her work with high-profile celebrities including the Kardashian-Jenner family, Hailey Bieber, and Gigi and Bella Hadid.

Chris Appleton, who is known for his sleek and modern hairstyles, often featuring high ponytails and polished finishes that have become trends in their own right.

Dimitris Giannetos, who has garnered attention for his innovative techniques and ability to create trendy looks, sharing his work on social media showcasing various styles and transformations.

And of course, the great Ken Pavés who is a beloved figure in the beauty and fashion world. I first met Ken when we worked with Lara Flynn Boyle and other celebrities in the early '90s. Our paths continued to cross as we collaborated on makeovers for Oprah's shows and often bumped into each other at QVC. I fondly remember attending Jennifer Lopez's performances, where I had the pleasure of shaping her brows, and sharing those beautiful moments with Ken.

In the early 2000s, we reconnected once again, this time around our favorite couple, Victoria and David Beckham. Ken is not only an extraordinary hairstylist but also a wonderful friend with an incredible sense of humor. I truly cherish the memories we've created together and hold our friendship dear to my heart. His clients include Jessica Simpson, Jennifer Lopez, and Eva Longoria.

The influence of top stylists is also undeniable, with visionaries like Law Roach, the "Image Architect," who blends different styles and aesthetics to create designs that are not only distinctive but tailored to reflect the individual personality of those he works with, including Zendaya and Ariana Grande. Monica Rose, known for her work with the Kardashians and Chrissy Teigen. Jessica Paster, whose clients include Anne Hathaway, Miranda Kerr, and more, is known for her elegant, tailored looks. Eric Archibald is known for blending trends with individual style, as showcased in his work with Megan Thee Stallion, Kerry Washington, Laverne Cox, Tessa Thompson, and Rihanna. Kate Young and Elizabeth Stewart redefine fashion standards, while the work of dynamic duo Rob Zangardi and Mariel Haenn has left a lasting impression on the fashion world and further cemented Jennifer Lopez's status as a style icon.

Social media creators inclusive of celebrities and influencers amplify these styles across platforms, like Stephanie Valentine, Camila Coelho, Bella Poarch, Khaby Lame, Charli D'Amelio, Addison Rae, Zach King, Mikayla Nogueira, Bach Buquen, Matteo Sinet, Alix Earle, Christen Dominique, Nikki La Rose, and many others.

Beauty editors play a pivotal role too. They are at the forefront of beauty trends, influencing products, styles, and iconic looks and disseminating ideas through platforms like *Allure*, *Byrdie*, *Vogue*, and others. Figures such as Sarah Kinonen at *Allure*; Hallie Gould at *Byrdie*; Faith Xue at Coveteur; Ariana Yaptangco at *Glamour*; Katie Intner at *Harper's Bazaar*; Asia Milia Ware at *New York* and *The Cut*; and Kiana Murden at *Vogue*. These editors and others bring styles to life and bridge the gap between celebrities and their fans.

Over the years, I've had the extraordinary opportunity to work with some of Hollywood's most remarkable actors and luminaries. As they prepared to embody their characters or roles, they'd often visit salons, where hairstyling, wigs, facial hair, specialty makeup artistry, and brow shaping all play crucial roles in transforming their expressions. Styling techniques allow actors and performers to fully immerse themselves in their roles on screen and captivate audiences. These men truly are masters of their craft. It's been a privilege to collaborate with such extraordinary artists and I cherish the unique memories from each experience.

Billy Bob Thornton is an actor I deeply admire. His dramatic transformations for roles are astounding, with his eyebrows often being a focal point. In films like *U Turn*, he's almost unrecognizable! We would often spend hours discussing the characters he would play, brainstorming the best ways to style his brows and hair to fit each role. Not many people know that he also worked as a solo singer-songwriter and with the band the Boxmasters. I still have a CD that he gave me, signed with his personal touch. His commitment to character and artistry is truly inspiring, and what an incredible artist he is!

When the late Donald Sutherland stepped into the salon, his presence was undeniable, instantly drawing everyone's attention. His deep, resonant voice and captivating aura left a lasting impression. I vividly recall him saying, "Anastasia, for my next role, I'll be playing a teacher." For this character, we aimed to present a gentler side of him. Instead of the striking, high-arched brows that typically signaled a formidable presence, we opted for a softer, more rounded shape. This subtle change transformed his expression, softening his features and infusing him with warmth and approachability. The new brow shape reflected the nurturing qualities of a dedicated educator, allowing his character to resonate with kindness and wisdom.

David Beckham would come to the salon to groom his brows for commercials and photo shoots. He was always gracious and approachable. I remember one time, when my colleague Alexandra asked to take a picture with him, he happily obliged, bringing such warm energy to everyone around him.

The late Val Kilmer's charisma was extraordinary. The excitement in the salon was palpable when the legendary actor came in to prepare for his role in *Wonderland*. The room fell silent as we tried to maintain a professional demeanor, but as soon as he left, everyone erupted in conversation. He left a lasting impression on all of us.

When I first met Ryan Seacrest, he was on the cusp of launching his career in show business, working at a local radio station. During our initial meeting, I noticed a prominent scar in his brows that caught my attention. I suggested that I could refine the shape to help soften its visibility. By carefully adjusting the arch and slightly reshaping the surrounding hairs, I was able to create a more balanced and harmonious brow line. This subtle enhancement not only diminished the appearance of the scar but also highlighted his expressive features, allowing his natural charisma to shine through. Ryan's journey in the entertainment industry is a remarkable testament to his incredible talent and relentless work ethic. His story of perseverance, passion, and the power of hard work proves that with determination and talent, one can achieve extraordinary heights.

Together, this interconnected community forms a pyramid of talent, with the stars at the top supported by a network of passionate creators. Each individual plays a vital role in the behind-the-scenes magic that gives Hollywood its sparkle. The passion of my peers inspires me, reminding me of that simple yet profound truth I learned in my mother's shop: Life's essence lies in honing our skills and sharing our gifts. Embracing this spirit of collaboration is the true magic of Hollywood, and it is what keeps the dream alive for all of us.

From a young age, I have yearned to learn, grow, and embrace the freedom to be my best self, flourishing among like-minded individuals who share the same aspirations. I envisioned Hollywood as the place where I would discover these inspiring people and witness my dreams come to life. This vision motivated me to leave Romania and make Hollywood my home. As I express in the pages of this book, it's crucial to surround yourself with those who inspire you and instill the belief that anything is possible—people whose dedication, achievements, expertise, and sustained success leave you in awe.

## Figures in our life, mentors, family members, or friends, often serve as role models. Their actions and achievements inspire admiration and aspiration.

Many people have impacted me along the way and changed my life for the better. Coming to America with nothing but a dream, I held tightly to the belief that hard work and vision could create a new future. One person who deeply influenced me is Michael Milken. His commitment to unlocking opportunity through the Milken Center for Advancing the American Dream is a powerful reminder that success is not just about what we build for ourselves but what we give back. Being part of this mission has fueled my passion to uplift others, and I hope my American success story encourages anyone chasing a dream to keep going. Many others who have impacted me started as clients and became close friends. I have been fortunate to know them during quiet moments and pivotal turning points. They work incredibly hard, relentlessly pursue their craft, seek to contribute to the world, and continuously strive to be better today than they were yesterday. For me, these talented individuals epitomize the American dream, which is a deeply personal journey, shaped by individual values, experiences, and goals, but it universally symbolizes hope, ambition, and the pursuit of a life filled with meaning and achievement. They each have accomplished this in their own way; they are each a true American success story. I am inspired by who they are and filled with admiration for their accomplishments.

# Jessica Alba

When I first met Jessica, she captivated me instantly. She is an extraordinary beauty. But it was her warm smile and infectious laugh that put me immediately at ease. She stands out from the crowd because of her genuine spirit. Whether she's lighting up the screen in a blockbuster film or speaking to you in private conversation, she has a unique energy that draws people in.

Her talent and accomplishments extend far beyond the roles she plays. As the cofounder of the Honest Company, she has made it her mission to provide safe, eco-friendly products. I've watched her pour her heart into this venture, driven by a desire to make the world better for our children.

One of the most meaningful experiences we shared was when Jessica introduced me to the nonprofit Baby2Baby. I treasure the time we spent together at their offices assembling care packages for families in need. She is always ready to help. Jessica and I and our daughters united with others to support those who lost their homes in the LA fires of 2025, giving back to the city we both cherish deeply.

Jessica juggles her thriving career and family life with grace that's nothing short of remarkable. I am constantly inspired by the tangible impact she makes on others with her kindness and empathy. I feel incredibly fortunate to call her my friend.

# Victoria Beckham

I met Victoria through Naomi. When Victoria moved to Los Angeles, Naomi introduced us, and soon after, Victoria began inviting me to her home, where I got to know the real Victoria Beckham, away from the spotlight. We quickly became close friends.

While some might perceive Victoria as serious due to her poised and stylish demeanor in photographs, what many don't realize is that she has an incredible sense of humor—an unmistakable British wit. Our evenings are always filled with laughter, especially when we're joined by our mutual friend, hairstylist Ken Pavés.

In my eyes, Victoria is a true superwoman. When we first met, she was raising three young boys and later on a baby girl, Harper, who she held close day and night. Remarkably, she didn't have a nanny—quite uncommon for working mothers with four children in Hollywood or anywhere else. At that time, she was building her fashion line, with her beauty business still on the horizon. I would be with her as she cradled Harper in her arms, surrounded by swatches of fabric, meticulously selecting colors and textures while still providing her assistant with detailed production notes. She was a whirlwind of energy, intelligence, and creativity. Watching her in action, I was constantly amazed by this petite, beautiful, and extraordinary woman.

Victoria and David are exceptional parents, raising their children to be polite and wonderful individuals. I often tell people that Victoria is my idol; my admiration for her knows no bounds. She has successfully built an incredible fashion and beauty empire while nurturing a loving family. On top of all that, she is the most supportive friend. If anyone embodies the golden ratio of life—achieving beauty, balance, and harmony—it is Victoria.

# Justin and Hailey Bieber

Justin and Hailey Bieber are truly remarkable individuals. I love to share a cup of tea with Justin, as I'm continually impressed by his deep understanding of Romanian culture. His talent is unparalleled, and his music resonates with such sensitivity and creativity. Attending one of his concerts was an unforgettable experience; the energy in the crowd was electric, with everyone singing along to every song. I proudly consider myself one of his biggest fans.

Hailey is equally captivating, and I admire her for launching a beauty line that reflects her knowledge and dedication to the craft. Whenever I shape her brows and she discusses every aspect of her business, it becomes clear just how involved she is in the process. Her marketing acumen is brilliant—who could forget her innovative partnership with Krispy Kreme to promote one of her products, or the creative launch of her lip gloss featured on an iPhone case. I am so proud of her. They both care deeply about supporting other young creators and entrepreneurs. It is a joy to know them and see them continue to share their considerable talents in new ways.

# Naomi Campbell

I've known Naomi since the very beginning of my career, and she holds a special place in my heart. She is one of the elite supermodels of our time, and it has been an incredible privilege to create moments of beauty and to care for someone who traveled the world nonstop. In those rare windows between flights, shows, and photo shoots, our brow appointments became cherished moments of stillness in her whirlwind life—brief interludes where she could pause and be cared for amid her relentless global schedule.

Whenever Naomi visits the salon, everything comes to a standstill. People whisper in awe, "Oh my God, that's Naomi Campbell." Her presence is unmistakable—a living masterpiece of perfect proportions and elegant lines. I've never seen anyone with a physique quite like hers. When we work together, I'm always struck by the classical perfection of her features, the canvas I'm so fortunate to enhance. If Michelangelo were alive today, the model he would use for the female counterpart to his *David*, his great sculpture, would be Naomi.

As our relationship evolved, due to her busy schedule, it often became more convenient to do her brows at my home, where she met and formed a close bond with my mother. What truly sets Naomi apart is her incredible kindness and the love she showered on me and my family. After a conversation with my mother, even if months or a year passed before we saw her again, Naomi would recall their discussion with incredible precision. It's astonishing to be remembered in such a personal way, especially considering the countless people Naomi meets. Her genuine interest in my family meant the world to me. Whenever we crossed paths, wherever we were in the world, she would always ask, "How is your mom? How is Mama?" It's remarkable.

Beyond her kindness, Naomi's legendary status in fashion comes alive on the runway—no one walks like Naomi. Her commanding presence and effortless grace captivate everyone in the room. I vividly remember attending Donatella Versace's first solo show at Milan Fashion Week in October 1997, showcasing the Spring/Summer 1998 collection shortly after Gianni Versace's passing. The fashion world was in mourning, and this event was both a debut for Donatella and a tribute to Gianni. Naomi, along with other supermodels, graced the runway, and I had the honor of doing her brows. I remained backstage, mesmerized as I watched her walk; she was simply breathtaking. Witnessing such an iconic moment in fashion is something I will never forget.

In recent years, since becoming a mother, Naomi has transformed in a truly special way. She welcomed her daughter and then later her son, embracing this new chapter with the same passion she brings to everything else. She now seems complete and filled with unconditional love. This new phase in her life has only added to her beauty and grace. Naomi continually inspires me with her heart, spirit, kindness, and the inner beauty that makes her shine. It's no wonder everyone calls her an icon—Naomi truly earns that title every day, both on and off the runway.

# Kris Jenner

Kris is like a sister to me. Although we grew up in very different environments, we both believe in hard work, the power of women, and the ability to figure things out. Most importantly, we believe in each other.

We first met years ago at Hollywood parties, where our paths would frequently cross. Kris began inviting Claudia and me to her Christmas celebrations, and I quickly discovered that she is an unparalleled host. With her large family, there were countless birthday parties and celebrations, and she graciously included us in the festivities. Our friendship blossomed from there. Kris possesses a stunning, effervescent beauty that captures attention. Everything about her is vivid, energetic, and magnetic, drawing people in. I genuinely admire what she has built for herself and her children. While I manage one child and one business, Kris expertly oversees six businesses, with all her kids finding success. I often wonder how she manages it all—she is truly amazing.

Once you get to know Kris, it becomes clear why she and her children are so successful. While her reputation as an innovator and marketing genius is well-known, I believe their achievements stem from other qualities as well. For one, they are incredibly kind. They treat their staff and everyone around them with respect and warmth. Kris has instilled a remarkable work ethic in her daughters, and they work tirelessly. She is exceptionally knowledgeable, disciplined, and focused. Her inner drive is an incredible force, perhaps her superpower. I have a strong drive as well, but hers is on another level, and I deeply respect that.

Kris also takes the time to mentor other entrepreneurs. We have spoken on numerous panels together about business, including the WWD Beauty CEO Summit alongside the esteemed Tommy Hilfiger. I can always rely on her to participate in my networking events for women entrepreneurs and leaders. We both share a desire to learn, grow, and stay attuned to emerging trends while giving back to the community. Every day, Kris strives to do her best for herself, her children, her customers, and the community at large. I am in awe of her accomplishments. Kris is a beautiful woman, a great leader, an incredible friend, and an everlasting source of inspiration for me.

# Kim Kardashian

Kim was the first Kardashian I met, and over time, I've come to know the entire family—Khloé, Kourtney, and Rob Kardashian, and Kylie and Kendall Jenner. Their influence extends beyond beauty. Their impact on fashion trends and social media has reshaped the industry, making them key players in contemporary pop culture.

When Kim first walked into the salon, everyone, myself included, paused to admire her. She possesses a charisma that radiates around her, a glow that draws you in. Yet, despite her beauty, she remains refreshingly down-to-earth. What struck me most during our first encounter, aside from her looks, was her genuine politeness toward everyone, from the receptionist to the specialists in the salon. Kim is remarkably punctual. She would drive from Calabasas to Beverly Hills, a journey that could take over an hour depending on traffic, yet she always arrived on time for her appointments. I admire this trait, as it reflects a deep respect for other people's time.

The entire Kardashian family shares these qualities; they are consistently polite and punctual. Their strong work ethic, instilled by their mother, Kris, is evident in everything they do. I respect how all the sisters are wonderful moms and friends to one another, showcasing a deep love and support that is truly admirable. Kylie is not just a successful businesswoman; she is also a fantastic mother and a loyal friend. Her ability to balance her thriving career with her role as a mom is inspiring. Kendall has become known for her striking features, which include perfectly shaped eyebrows that enhance her expressive eyes. Her high cheekbones and defined jawline further accentuate her beauty, making her a standout figure in the fashion industry. Her versatility in looks and ability to carry various styles, from natural to glamorous, showcases her unique charm and allure. She and her sisters bring joy and positivity into the lives of those around them. I feel so fortunate to call all of them my friends.

Kim is always at the forefront of beauty and style, possessing a clear vision for what she wants. She expresses gratitude to the behind-the-scenes professionals who help bring her vision to life and has been instrumental in supporting and elevating the careers of makeup artists and stylists. Seeing her on the red carpet, I am always captivated by the stunning image she has created. Let's face it, her brows are the most requested brow shape ever!

I'll never forget the day she came to my salon just to surprise one of my interns who adored her. There were no cameras or publicity—just a heartfelt gesture that created a lifelong memory. Not everyone would take that extra step, but she does, and that means a lot. Ultimately, it's all about love. In my experience, truly successful individuals recognize their place within a community, and Kim embodies this sensibility alongside her talent and hard work. She is beautiful in every way.

# Eva Longoria

I had the pleasure of meeting Eva Longoria during her time on *The Young and the Restless*. From the outset, her striking beauty and remarkable talent suggested she was destined for greatness in Hollywood. She truly became a household name with her iconic role in the hit TV series *Desperate Housewives*.

Eva's contributions to the entertainment industry are only matched by her dedication to social causes, particularly her advocacy for the Hispanic community and women's rights. Not only has she thrived as an actress, but she has also made her mark as a producer, director, and philanthropist.

Her vibrant personality truly brightens every gathering. Eva has a deep passion for cooking, particularly Mexican cuisine, which beautifully showcases her heritage. It's always a joy to watch her in the kitchen, preparing delicious meals for us after Ken styles her hair. I'll shape her brows, and then Elan Bongiorno, her talented makeup artist, will perfect the look. We often wrap up our time together with a drink—her favorite tequila, Casa del Sol— because she knows how to whip up a killer margarita.

Together with Victoria Beckham, Ken Pavés, and Charlene Roxborough Konsker, we have shared countless memorable moments, whether at each other's homes or industry events. One unforgettable experience was attending Victoria Beckham's fashion show in Paris in September 2024, alongside Sofía Vergara. We sat in the front row, enveloped in a breathtaking atmosphere surrounded by iconic figures from the fashion industry, including the legendary Anna Wintour from *Vogue*. It was truly a magical experience, immersed in the glamour and creativity that define the world of high fashion.

Everything about Eva radiates warmth, generosity, and joy. She uplifts and inspires everyone she encounters, including me. I feel grateful to be part of her circle and to have witnessed her remarkable rise to stardom and the significant impact she continues to make.

# Jennifer Lopez

My appreciation for Jennifer Lopez transcends her status as a superstar; it is deeply rooted in our friendship and the journey we've shared. From the moment I met her through her publicist, Karynne Tencer, I sensed that Jennifer was destined for greatness. She has not only dazzled the world with her exceptional talent and stunning beauty but has also embodied the qualities of loyalty and friendship that are rare in the entertainment industry. Our bond was forged during her early days, especially when she took on the role of Selena. I had the privilege of visiting her on set, where I shaped her brows, witnessing firsthand the dedication and passion she poured into her craft. It was exhilarating to be part of that journey, driving through the iconic Paramount Studios, knowing we were both on the cusp of something remarkable.

As the years have passed, I've watched in awe as Jennifer has evolved into an even more captivating figure. Each new era reveals a different facet of her sophistication and unique style, and her ability to reinvent herself continually inspires me. On Oscar days, working alongside the talented Oribe and Scott Barnes, I felt immense pride in contributing to her stunning looks, knowing that I played a small part in her transformation into a true red-carpet icon.

Beyond her dazzling presence, what truly sets Jennifer apart is her unwavering determination. I recall her performing while pregnant with her twins, showcasing an incredible blend of talent, resilience, and work ethic. Jennifer continues to evolve in her career, making her a true force in the entertainment industry.

Jennifer remains not only a star in the limelight but also a cherished friend. I look forward to witnessing the next chapters of her extraordinary career, knowing that our friendship will endure amid the glitz and glamour.

# Sharon Stone

Everything about Sharon Stone is extraordinary. She started as my client and then became a close friend. I vividly remember the first time she sat in my chair. My daughter, Claudia, approached to share something with me, and as Sharon opened her eyes, Claudia exclaimed, "You have the most beautiful features I have ever seen in my life." It was a true statement; Sharon, a former model, possesses the most exquisite features—her nose, eyes, eyebrows, and overall face are nothing short of perfection. Few women achieve such a perfect balance and proportion, but she is undoubtedly one of them.

The first time I visited her home was when she was nominated for an Oscar. She entered the room like a diva, a living goddess. I had the honor of doing her brows while she donned a stunning black Versace dress. Two seamstresses from Versace were there, visibly nervous in her presence, showcasing just how much of a star she is.

I was impressed by the grandeur of her home, reminiscent of the Hermitage Museum in Saint Petersburg, Russia. Just like Catherine the Great, who started acquiring art and artifacts early in life, Sharon has exquisite taste; every piece of furniture is carefully chosen and reflects her unique style. She possesses a sophisticated, worldly sensibility and a profound appreciation for art. As you walk through her home, you can't help but admire her extensive collection of paintings. Remarkably, with the earnings from her first film, she purchased works by Jean-Michel Basquiat long before he became famous. Sharon herself is an incredible artist, painting regularly and traveling to showcase her work. Her talents are truly multifaceted.

Then there's her library. My literature teacher in Romania once told us, "Your library should represent who you are. When someone looks at your books, they will know you." Sharon's library embodies this philosophy, filled with an impressive array of important literature. I fell in love with her just by perusing the titles on her shelves.

Now, we share a close friendship. No matter where we are in the world, we always stay connected and support each other. I am truly grateful to have such a brilliant, creative, and endlessly fascinating person in my life to call my friend.

# Sofía Vergara

I affectionately call Sofía Vergara "My Favorite Neighbor," and let me tell you, our connection is something truly special—a rare gem that I hold dear. The first time we met, we went out for dinner at a nearby restaurant, and from that moment, it was like we had hit the conversational jackpot! Our dynamic is a vibrant exchange of energy, admiration, and ideas. Sofía has shown me that Colombians and Romanians have a lot in common; sometimes I think Macedonians and Romanians must be like Colombian cousins. We share a similar outlook on life—we love food, treasure friendships, and relish meaningful conversations with other women. For us, loyalty and dedication to our passions are nonnegotiable.

What many don't realize is that Sofía is not just breathtakingly gorgeous; she's also naturally hilarious. While people may know her as Gloria from *Modern Family*, that same humor shines through in real life. Her infectious joy brings laughter and fun to everyone around her. But don't let that fool you—she's incredibly smart and serious when it counts. Sofía has built a successful beauty empire, launched her own fragrance and clothing lines, and even designed a stunning collection of furniture. Talk about multitalented!

Sofía has faced her share of challenges in life, yet she embraces every moment with incredible vitality. My daughter and I have been lucky enough to be swept up in her whirlwind of joy. We've celebrated Thanksgivings and birthdays together and even traveled through Europe. Our time spent cooking and chatting at each other's homes reminds me of the big family gatherings I cherished growing up in Romania.

I was absolutely thrilled when she made history as the first Latina actress nominated for an Emmy in a lead role for her powerful performance in Netflix's *Griselda*. The transformation she underwent for that role was nothing short of remarkable. Attending the Emmys and Golden Globes to celebrate with my friend was an experience that touched my heart.

Sofía continually lifts me up with her brilliance and her unique approach to life. I strive to surround myself with people I love, can learn from, and who bring joy into my life—Sofía embodies all that and more. I truly love her and her wonderful family.

Each of these immensely talented artists, creatives, innovators and the many others whom I have known or met along the way contribute to the magic of Hollywood. What I've come to understand is that admiring others is invaluable to setting your own course in life. The people that surround us every day—mentors, family members, or friends—often serve as role models. Their actions and achievements inspire admiration and aspiration. When you see other people you admire striving for excellence in their work, their art, their life, you can't help but try to do the same. I have been enriched by their stories and by how they navigate the challenges we all encounter, as well as their hard-earned triumphs. I feel profoundly grateful for their presence in my life and for the impact they have had on my journey.

# Acknowledgments

There are so many people I wish to thank for their help, support, and encouragement. First and foremost, I want to take a moment to talk about my daughter, Claudia, who is truly my greatest achievement. She is a beautiful and brilliant young woman, and I couldn't be prouder of everything she has accomplished.

Claudia grew up with a unique set of challenges, often like a Spartan warrior, with a mother who worked tirelessly and wasn't always present when she needed me the most. She started school without speaking a word of English, and I empathize deeply with the struggles faced by so many immigrant children. Navigating a new environment is never easy, especially when surrounded by peers who can sometimes be unkind. There were days when she would walk home from school because I was at work and unable to pick her up. When she attended Beverly Hills High School, she didn't want me to drop her off or pick her up because the other kids would tease her about the car I was driving, while their parents were in Porsches or BMWs. On the days I was able to drive her to or from school, I would park several streets away to respect her wishes.

I remember a time when Claudia was working the front desk during her school vacation for some extra money. One of her classmates had a Chanel bag. Claudia admired it, and her friend suggested she should get one, to which she replied, "I don't have the money to buy an expensive bag." The classmate responded, "But your mom is Anastasia; she can afford it."

Every penny we had was invested back into the business, and I always emphasized to Claudia that at her age, it was more important to eat healthily, work out, and not worry about expensive clothes or bags. She never argued; it took a lot for a beautiful girl to forgo what many of her peers had, yet she never complained.

As she began working with me, she applied everything she learned to her job. I'm so glad she chose to join me; she witnessed firsthand the hard work and sacrifices it took to pursue our dreams. There were days when she struggled to see a brighter future, but she trusted my guidance, and for that, I am immensely grateful. I too had moments of discouragement, but I knew I couldn't give up. Every time I looked back, I reminded myself that all our sacrifices had to bear fruit.

Claudia is wise and intelligent; working in the salon provided her with invaluable experiences and lessons. By the time she transitioned to the corporate office, she had developed a newfound confidence and a strong desire to learn and grow. She saw a path illuminated with potential, and as she began to understand the business, she transformed into a new version of herself.

One remarkable quality about Claudia is her ability to remember every mistake she has ever made, ensuring she never repeats them. She has evolved into an incredible strategist, always considering various scenarios—both good and bad—and finding effective solutions.

Today, Claudia is one of the most interesting and influential figures in the beauty industry. Her passion is evident in her work ethic, as she puts her heart into everything she does.

If you ask her what brings her joy, she would mention her grandmother Dada, her boyfriend, and her three beloved dogs. But above all, her work is what she cherishes most. I am so proud of who she has become; she is my biggest accomplishment in life, and she means everything to me.

I also want to express my deepest gratitude to all my customers, clients, friends, employees, advisers, and family who have been part of my journey. I've been supported by so many incredible people, too many to name without missing someone. Thank you all from the bottom of my heart. This isn't just my story. It's a reflection of *your* American dream too. Thank you for constantly inspiring me and reminding me what's possible.

And there are others too who I wish to thank in the creation of this book.

First, thank you to Desiree Gruber, who believed in me from the beginning. I value our long friendship.

Thank you to my literary agent, Heidi Krupp, for championing this project from the start. I am grateful for your brilliant advice and for steering this book to the right publishing home. You are a powerhouse!

Thank you to Claudia Riemer Boutote of Red Raven Studio for your invaluable assistance in shaping this manuscript and helping me to bring my story to life with clarity and heart. I'm grateful for your keen editorial insights, writing expertise, and wise suggestions throughout the creation of this book that made it possible.

I want to thank my publisher, Adrian Zackheim, who recognized the potential of this book and welcomed me into the fold at Portfolio. You are my dream publisher!

Thank you to Lydia Yadi—your early readings of the manuscript, astute edits, and feedback helped to shape the vision for the book. To my editor Megan McCormack, who came in midstream without missing a beat. Thank you to Jennifer Heuer, art director, for the elegant cover.

And to the entire Portfolio team, thank you for your hard work and dedication.